Charles Reid Barnes

Correspondence with Walter Deane, 1886-1909

Charles Reid Barnes

Correspondence with Walter Deane, 1886-1909

ISBN/EAN: 9783337393953

Printed in Europe, USA, Canada, Australia, Japan

Cover: Foto ©ninafisch / pixelio.de

The Botanical Gazette.

EDITORS:

JOHN M. COULTER,
WABASH COLLEGE, CRAWFORDSVILLE, IND.

CHARLES R. BARNES,
PURDUE UNIVERSITY, LAFAYETTE, IND.

J. C. ARTHUR,
AGRIC. EXPER. STATION, GENEVA, N. Y.

Cambridge, Mass.
July 8. 1886.

My dear Deane:- Your p.c. came a day or so ago, but it has been so <u>infernally</u> hot (I use the expression in its etymological significance) that I have not had the courage to answer it by lamplight and have had no time in the day. This morning I was unable to sleep by reason of the heat, so I am up long before breakfast and find myself after a bath moderately comfortable clad only in shirt, breeches and stockings. But the sky is cloudless, the sun coppery and the light breeze far from cool already (7 A.M.) and so I look forward to another swelter. I went in to Boston yesterday, <u>not</u> on a pleasure trip I assure you, and this did not add to my comfort. While there I bought the forceps you wanted. The other things, razor and glass-ware require no selecting and I thought you could get them as easily and as well as I.

I got a very neat little pair of forceps for 45¢.—

The school of botany comes on swimmingly— There are upwards of 30 in the class and Dr. Goodale expresses himself as highly pleased with the way they take hold—

You may say to Mrs. Deane that I know now why this mansion is considered by the neighbors as unusually elastic— We have six in the house beside myself and the usual family! The mistresses of the house have given up their room and the little tower room (6×6 or thereabouts) is occupied— Where the Misses S— sleep deponent saith not! Besides that Mrs. C. O. Thompson and sons dine here—— We have gay times now and the conversation is often spirited— I am daily astonished at the amount of nonsense (bosh! to use a more expressive word) educated people can talk about subjects of which they are incompetent judges! But I cannot enter into particulars in a letter. Come down and see me before I go, which I now expect to do on Tuesday next. My wife & mother have arrived safe in N. Va—— My kindest regards to Mrs. D——

Sincerely Yours C. R. B.—

The Botanical Gazette.
EDITORS:
JOHN M. COULTER,
WABASH COLLEGE, CRAWFORDSVILLE, IND.
CHARLES R. BARNES,
PURDUE UNIVERSITY, LAFAYETTE, IND.
J. C. ARTHUR,
AGRIC. EXPER. STATION, GENEVA, N. Y.

Cambridge, Mass-
July 11. 1886-

My dear Deane:- I enclose the forceps and hope they will prove serviceable and convenient-

I spent yesterday packing up so that my hands are stiffened up this A.M. by the unusual handling of hammer and the moving of weighty boxes- Whereas I came to Cambridge with two small boxes, I ship away three large ones; one so heavy that I can barely "up-end" it- That is my box of books, paper, and microscopes-

It is barely possible that I shall not go until Wednesday P.M.- I bought a flannel shirt at Jordan Marsh & Co's a day or two ago and if they are closed Monday on acc't of Mr. Marsh's

Wednesday for I want to exchange it for a smaller size –

Will write you if I stay and possibly you can come down –

Regards to Mrs D

Ever faithfully yrs,

C R Barnes

Cambridge, July 12.

My dear Drane:—I have decided not to go until Wednesday P.M. If you've nothing else to do run down and see me off—I shall go at 4:30 or 6.—Don't know which yet.—Yrs C. R. B.

UNITED STATES

POSTAL CARD

RIDGE STA. JUL 14 MASS.

Nothing but the address to be on this side.

W. Deane, Esq.
Concord,
Mass.—
Near the Old Manse—

where I checked the same packages before starting for Kansas. ~~Thank you~~ —

As soon as possible after greeting the relatives I started out to see the people at the Agric. Dept. I went first to see Wiley the Chemist who was formerly our Prof. of Chemistry at Purdue and came from my native county, Jefferson, and was ~~[illegible]~~ educated at the same College, Hanover. Then I went up to see Scribner and Vasey, the former of whom asked me to dine with him the next day. I then walked back with him as far as the Capitol and had a very pleasant talk. The evening was rainy so I spent it in-doors. The next day was a beautiful one and I put it in faithfully in seeing as much of W. as possible. I went to the N.W. section, where the beautiful residences & statues are, then to the Treasury where I called on the 3rd Auditor, Jno. S. Williams, a Lafayette

Substitute "Green Spring Run" for Springfield in the address I gave you — the rest remaining the same

"Fair View" near
Green Spring Run, W. Va.
July 22. 1886 —

My dear Deane;

Leisure comes to me this A.M. for writing; nay, more; I feel the need of employing my time for a while; hence this letter.

As I wrote you I left Boston on Wednesday evening via the Stonington Line for N.Y. I took the Stonington in preference to the Fall River because its boats are due in N.Y. an hour earlier than the others and I wanted to make sure of catching the train for Washington that my mother and wife missed, viz. the "Southern Express", rather than the one half an hour later, the "Washington Mail"; which gets into W.

2 hours later. I accomplished my object comfortably and had a speedy ride to W. I hoped to enjoy a moonlight ride on the Sound but the night was cloudy, almost rainy and in the morning as we came into N.Y. harbor the rain came down in sheets. Between showers, however, and from protected parts of the boat I enjoyed what I never tire of seeing the various interesting "sights" of the East River and Harbor. You know what they are and how entertaining they are. After ferrying to Jersey City I had time to get a "square meal" at the Restaurant. I breakfasted on a whole porter-house steak and delicious bread and butter for which I paid 30¢! Think of that for a rail road restaurant!

I got in to Washington at 1:40 after a delightful ride, entirely free from dust or cinders because of the heavy rain of the previous night and the strong wind which blew off the smoke. We stopped only at Newark, Trenton, Phil^a, Wilmington, the Susquehanna bridge and Baltimore.

After cleaning up at the station I had my first introduction to Washington prices. I went to the parcel room to leave my hand baggage and as the young man checked it he remarked "30¢". I said "What?" He replied "30¢". I asked, "Do you mean that you want 30¢ for keeping that stuff for a day?" and when he said that he did I concluded that I could take care of it cheaper than that, so I carried it with me to my uncle's where I stopped while there. It made more impression perhaps because it was in such striking contrast to the Providence station

I get back to Ridgedale where we make our headquarters.—

~~Kn~~ I must postpone telling you of my mts. climbing and collecting until another letter. Excuse the looks of this epistle please for I'm writing on my lap (a thing which I despise to do!) and with a poor pen— "Haste and a bad pen" — the usual excuse for poor chirography!—

My wife sends regards to yourself & Mrs. L.— to whom also my regards— Mother has gone down to Winchester, Va. & will be back today & join us here, whence we go back to Ridgedale on Saturday—

Write— Yours ever C.R.Barnes

Patent Office, Capitol and Nat. Museum. At the latter I called on Ward and Knowlton who seemed to remember your visit with pleasure. By the time I got through talking with them it was time to join Scribner, so I went to the Ag. building and at four o'clock we went to the B & O. depot and took the train for Hyattsville, a suburb of W. where S. lives. Had a pleasant visit with him. He has a wife and 2 children, one 4 years old and one 14 mos, both boys. He showed me his grasses and many of his drawings and told me of his work. He also told me of his plans for the year in the mycological work of the department. Since the 1st of July his position has changed

He is no longer "Assistant Botanist" but is in charge of the Mycologic Section and reports direct to the Commr. This change he sought as it will probably improve his salary and make him independent of Vasey who seems to be jealous of his grass work. I cannot tell you the whole story but a single instance will suffice. Pringle sent S. his grasses to determine. Vasey hearing of it wrote to P. that he wished him to send his grasses to him (Vasey)! From S.'s remarks I judge that V. has made it rather unpleasant for S. for a year or more. It's too bad! But I'd rather trust Scribner in grasses twice over than Vasey. V. is going out this summer to Arizona & N. Mex. collecting and investigating the question of sowing some of the grasses for forage on the drier, "un-irrigable" portions of those regions. Just what he expects to accomplish by his visit I do not see, though there is doubtless great good to be accomplished ~~by~~ if the plan is feasible. He can see how dry the region is, but beyond that I do not know what he can do. Scribner is working on the Muhlenbergias now and finds them very puzzling he says. His time is limited to nights and Sundays and so progress is slow. He has all the Muhlenbergias from Cambridge. He doesn't think much of Eatonia Dudleyi (Vasey in Bot. Gaz. June) and considers that there are only 2 Eatonias viz = Pennsylvanica ? and obtusata ? (These are the ones I believe, tho' I'm not sure.) Beal's book on Grasses is, I learn from him, about 1/2 in type. It is being printed in Lansing! at an office where they can hardly hold a signature in type at once! I'm sorry to hear that, for poor typog-

Rees's Tannery,
Mineral Co., W. Va.,
July 31, 1886.

My dear Deane:-

I want in this letter to tell you something of our visit in the mountains. This last day of July is a rainy one. It finds us snugly ensconced in a cousin's room in the New Creek Valley of Mineral Co. — But I will begin at the beginning.

My first stop was in Hampshire Co., Eleven miles from Green Spring, on the South Branch R.R., a feeder of the B. & O. "Ridgedale," the name of the homestead — all the farms in this country are named — is an estate of 3000 acres lying in the bottoms of the South Branch of the Potomac and on the various ridges which constitute the Patterson Creek Mts. Of course the largest part of the land is on th...

tate has been in the hands of the Washington family ever since the country was settled, i.e., about 100 years. The South Branch and the S.B. R.R. both run through the farm. The R.R. crosses the river on a long trestle and bridge half a mile from the house, and then passes with in 400 yards of the door. Of course this railroad which is only 16 m. long is solely a feeder of the B.+O. and as there is but one train on the road they are very accommodating to the people along the line. I got off at the very door, so to speak, and found my wife awaiting me. Our mail came twice a day, the conductor bringing it from Green Spring or Springfield (as it happened to be directed) and throwing it off at the switch. Moreover we had the Baltimore morning paper on the same day and, though so far in the mountains, this made us feel quite "in the world." The house is a huge brick, built just "befo' de wah" on a scale as to size that is almost appalling. One ascends a dozen broad steps to a wide porch which extends across the front and enters, through a single door fully as wide as your double front doors, a hall about the width of your parlor, which extends through the house. Right and left are four rooms connected by folding doors and above the same number of chambers. At the back of the house is a large Ell and porch for the kitchen and rooms for the hands. Of course there is the usual accompaniment of outbuildings, milk house, meat house etc. The negro quarters further back and to the side are going to rack. What would strike a Pennsylvanian as particularly lacking is the accommodation for crops and horses. The stables and barns are small and in an almost ruined state, though the granaries are in good condition. You know in Pa. and many parts of the West a man has a fine barn, if he lives in a pig-sty himself.

The Family at [illegible]

of "Aunt Sallie" Washington, the mother, a beautiful old lady, and an unmarried ~~brother~~ son and daughter. The son carries on the "place" and the daughter the house. Of course such an estate requires considerable management. They have about a dozen "hands" and as many "tenants" to look after. 27 work horses are in constant use, besides riding horses and colts innumerable. The cattle on the ridges have to be looked after, the harvests on the tilled land cared for and shipments of grain, wood and bark kept going. "Bob" Washington is a "pusher" though, and keeps the grass well worn under his feet. Here is a sample. He went to Romney one day leaving orders with the men to fill a box-car with wheat. He got back at midnight and found they had put 250 bu. in during the day! The car was to go on the 7:30 AM train and he routed those men out at 4 o'clock and before train time they put in 350 bushels more! He ships a car-load (10 tons = 10 cords) of bark every day to a tannery at Pawpaw on the main line B.&O. This bark is one of the principal sources of revenue from the ridge lands hereabouts. It is the bark of Quercus Prinus var. acuminata, called Chestnut Oak here. The trees are felled in spring "when the sap runs" (i.e. when the cambium cells are forming) and stripped from the trunk and branches and piled. During the summer and autumn it is ready for shipment, being then thoroughly dry. The wood is in most cases left to rot, as there is no market for it and it could hardly be gotten down off the mts. if there were. Bob has cut about 120,000 trees (=50,000 cords cleared) this season! It seems a great waste, doesn't it? You ought to see some of those "bark roads"! In many places locking the hind-wheels and putting on a "rough-lock" (which cuts deep into the soil) is not sufficient to hold back the wagon and they then resort to felling a small tree and hitching that to the back end of the wagon! In other places even this fails. Then they tie a rope to the hind axle and taking a "hitch" round a tree let the wagon slide down!! You would hardly believe that a loaded wagon could get down [illegible] that way!

After staying but a day or two at Ridgedale we all went down the river visiting other relatives, stopping first at "Pleasant Retreat" two miles from Springfield, where I had my first mountain climbing. The farm and house of this grand-uncle lie in a bend of the river, and across the neck of the bend lie the Jersey Mts, whose highest point is at this place. So one ~~morn~~ing I climbed to the summit. The "climb" was comparatively easy as an alleged road goes over the summit here. The road is a cleared track, rough, rocky and gullied by the rains, with a grade like that of the tiled tower of Trinity! I took it slowly though and regaled myself on the blue-berries which lined the "road". The view at the top certainly repaid me however. Far to the east, across the Valley of Va. lay the Blue Ridge, showing only in faint lines through the gaps of the Great North Mts which form the boundary of the state. Between Jersey and Gt. North lay Sandy Ridge, North River Mts and Spring Gap Mts. ~~Down~~ Up the valley lay innumerable ridges, with the smaller valleys covered with wheat and corn fields, with here and there cleared fields even at the summits of the hills. To the west the Patterson Crk. Mts. cut off the ~~view~~ view. Through the main valley the South Branch snakes its way, making a double S just below me. It was certainly beautiful!

After a week's stay here and at "Ferndale" (where there were 5 lively girls) and at "Fair view", we returned to Ridgedale where we staid several days, coming over here yesterday.

I don't know that I told you that my mother's family all came from this region. Her grandfather, John Lyle, preached for years at Springfield and is buried there. My grandmother was born there, but the whole family removed to Ky. when she was 3 years old shortly after the death of her father. Mother of course has been much interested in hunting up the family history and in seeing places she has heard the traditions of. She went over to Winchester to see Greenwood the estate of the Emigrant from County Down, North Ireland, Samuel Glass, who founded her -

in this country. It lies about 3 miles from Winchester at the head of Opequon Creek. The creek heads in a huge spring on the premises, a spring so strong that 200 yards down it runs a mill and has done so for a century! She brot a jar of water from it that she is going to take to relatives in Marion where she will go from here.

In studying up the family history and connections we find quite a coincidence. Mary and I are, on opposite sides of the house, exactly the same kin to Mrs. Judge Armstrong of Romney, viz. second cousins, once removed! You will at once see from what I have told you that my wife and I are both __F. F. V.'s__!

From Romney yesterday we came by stage, for the sake of the scenery, which was certainly beautiful. We are now on New Creek, 5 miles from Keyser. The Creek runs by the front of the house and the New Creek Mts. rise abruptly on the other side. Behind us lies the Front Ridge of the Alleghany Mts. Close by the house is a large tannery (sole leather) [illegible] as is almost everything in sight, by our host, Mr. James Rees. The house is delightful with almost city appointments and furnishing. It is heated by waste steam from the tannery and has bath-room and set bowls supplied by the large spring which furnishes water for the tannery. Two cousins are visiting here with us, and there are 3 girls in the house besides. We shall stay here until Thursday or Friday of next week when we go home. I think I shall go home with my wife as I can get back to Buffalo almost as cheaply as I can go from here, because of the reduction I get on round trip. By the way, notice that your fare (round trip) to B. is @ 1½¢ per mile, not 1⅓ fare. I think that will be even cheaper. Don't fail to come.

I forgot to tell you of my trip up Middle Ridge from Ridgedale. Cousin Etta Washington and I went up on horseback. We took the wrong road and it wound up in a bark camp, so we climbed ⅓ the way up the Mt. through the brush, over logs and ...

tween trees hung with grape-vines. It was tough work for the horses and quite difficult for us to keep from being pulled off but we got through to daylight and found along the top an easy way to the summit. The view was finer than anything I have ever seen. I cannot undertake to describe it. I don't believe the White Mts. can beat it anywhere. Get your largest map of W. Va. and find a point 2 miles west of the South Branch and 4 miles north of Romney. From there our view included the Front Ridge of the Alleghanies on the west, Cumberland, Md. on the N. the Gt. North Mts. on the east and nearly to Moorefield on the South! In no direction was the view obstructed! Oh! it was magnifique!--

I must reserve botanical matters till I see you. Suffice it to [illegible] that I have collected a good many mosses, tho' not so many as I expected, because we have been "going" so. I shall get some here.

My wife sends her regards to "the Deanes". Include mine to Mrs. D.

As ever, Sincerely yrs

[illegible]

Note Authority [illegible]

PURDUE UNIVERSITY,
LAFAYETTE, IND.

Sept. 8. 1886.

My dear Deane:-

Here I am just settling down to work again. I have been far too busy for the last month to write. I cannot well tell you how disappointed I was that you finally failed to materialize at Buffalo. That seemed so definitely settled when I parted from you that I did not doubt that I should soon see you again. I think you deserve that I make your mouth water in thinking of the good things you missed by not coming. We had a grand time. At no previous meeting have there been so many botanists and never have such elaborate preparations been made for their entertainment. To be sure some of the stand-byes were not on hand — e.g. Bessey, Halsted et al. — but there were enough to insure a good meeting.

I joined Coulter at Indianapolis and we journeyed together, reaching B. at 8 o'clock Wednesday A.M. We went at once to the Ass'n quarters, the High School building and after registering, etc., spent the morning in meeting the botanists and getting acquainted with strangers, especially those of the local Club. At noon we went out to our abiding place, Mr. Day's, in company with Scribner, who was invited to dinner that day. Arthur was already established at Mr. Day's and he piloted us. We three —

PURDUE UNIVERSITY,
LAFAYETTE, IND.

of the Gazette — and "our special artist" (i.e., our stenographer (ahem!)) were delightfully and most hospitably entertained by Mr. Day. You may think that the Gazette is "flying high" to indulge in the luxury of a stenographic report! Well, so she is!! But it didn't cost much! Of course as we were "on the go" so much we saw comparatively little of Mr. Day. He is a most genial gentleman and seemed to take great pleasure in having us at his house. Sunday afternoon we went across the river with him and strolled along the Canada shore as far as Old Fort Erie. There was nothing in my line to be gathered but Coulter and Arthur picked up some nice things, among others Calamintha glabella and Triglochin — palustre I think. It was the little or

Wednesday afternoon was spent in sociability and in listening to the address of the Vice-President (Bowditch) (Section 7.) on "What is nerve force?" Wednesday evening we went to a reception at Dr & Mrs. Wright's where a good time and a good feed (and a good drink for drinkers) was assured - Thursday A.M. at 9 the Bot. Club held its first meeting - As a full account of these proceedings will appear in the Gazette I will not weary you beforehand with it - Thursday P.M. the Ass'n went down the River to Grand Island to the grounds of the Falconwood Club - Here was a charming boat ride, a delightful club-house and grounds and an elegant lunch - "all free, and welcome" - You may be sure we enjoyed the day much and had a specially good time on the boat. A number of us, wishing to get home earlier took the private steam yacht of the Club for the homeward ride. By the time we got dressed in the evening the time had arrived for the botanical reception at Mr. Day's house. About 250 invitations were issued and I think fully as many were there. We had a charming evening, free from all formality and full of good fellowship, a "swell" supper and a happy time generally! See Bot. Gaz. for particulars. — Friday P.M. from 4–6 we spent at the garden party at Mr. & Mrs. Rumsey's. To say that they have the finest private grounds I ever saw may not convey much of an idea to your mind, but I cannot enter further into particulars. The members of the A.A.A.S. amused themselves in strolling or rowing about the lake, or, sitting in groups under the magnificent trees, talked and watched the plashing fountains and gurgling springs. Finally they all sauntered near enough to a large marquee to sniff the coffee, a reminder of the ever-present feed which all took with charming unanimity. All this, bear in mind was in the back yard of a house in the center of the city! It beats my back yard all to pieces!

Saturday everybody (nearly) went on the Niagara Excursion, very few taking the Chautauqua trip. The botanists I suppose all went to the Falls, as they so expressed themselves in the club the previous morning. We wandered over Goat Island and botanized freely, spite of the ubiquitous sign warning us not to "cut, break or otherwise

injure any of the plants."
Hypericum Kalmianum, Fissidens grandifrons and Gymnostomum calcareum and curvirostrum are the special plants of the Falls. I got the Fissidens and Gym. curvirostrum tho' Mr. Rau and Mrs. Britton failed to find the former.

Sunday P.M. we went with Mr. D. as I before related. I forgot to say that on Friday night we (editorial & literally, in this case) invited about a dozen of the jolliest of the botanists up to our rooms and we did have a gay time. There were Bebb and Beal and Scribner and Spalding and Davis and Sargent and several others. Mr. Day came up, and between botanical talk, cigars and good stories you may imagine that no time went to waste!!

on the steamer Huntress to Point Abino, a sandy point 15 miles from B. on the Canada shore, backed by a range of dunes. It rained for an hour and delayed our landing some what but as soon as it ceased the sand was perfectly dry and we rambled around for an hour and a half. I collected nothing, but the party who went with Mr. Day and were after phanerogams got a good lot of things. By the time set for leaving the rain began again, but ceased before we landed in B. On the way back a fine spread was laid by the ladies of the local Club, which gave full opportunity for joke and laugh. I made some exceedingly pleasant acquaintances and I am sure all had a jolly time –

Tuesday A.M., at 6, Coulter and

I left. What was done on that day beside holding the usual meetings I do not know.

To say that you missed it by not coming is drawing it very mild indeed! You see I want to make you feel just as badly as I possibly can, so that you will be sure to come to the next meeting. Where it is to be is not yet decided, but it will probably be still nearer to you, possibly at N.Y. or Saratoga. Make your plans to do so now and just tell Mrs. D. that you are going and that she is not to attempt even to persuade you to the contrary.

Since getting back from Buffalo I have been working like a "hired man" in getting settled in the house we have taken. We are now in shape, just, and [illegible] you could call on us where we could return some of your bountiful hospitality.

College opens auspiciously with increase in every class. I think we shall have 350 students this year.

Of course I kept looking for letters from you. While I was so busy you were idling(?) your time at Rye Beach! Why did'nt you write again, you rascal? Are you going to exchange letters with me merely? What a way! Don't! Write often—

My wife would send her regards I know were she at my elbow, so I make bold to do it for her. With my own kindest regards to Mrs. Deane, believe me

Ever sincerely yours,

C. R. Barnes

PURDUE UNIVERSITY,
LAFAYETTE, IND.

September 23. 1886.

My dear Deane:-

Who is Towne, anyhow? I did not know that Cambridge boasted of such a crank! Why did I not have opportunity to meet him at the houses of some of the distinguished scientists? Too bad! For then I might have had explained to me what the "Electrical beating in of oxygen atoms" meant and how all this electrical energy "drives the wheels of plant life". Now that's what we're all longing to know. Alas! that the only man who knows what drives the wheels of life escaped me! But I can console myself, I suppose with the supposition that I should have been like the "eminent head &c" who was "good only for the study of facts and the most direct inferences from them"! That's capital! Doesn't it sound like Farlow? Whoever he was he was loth to part with his "totally false knowledge" [sic] on plant physiology—

I'm surprised that the Transcript would admit such stuff to its columns.—

Sept. 24. — I shall often have to write my letters in installments, I fear, as interruptions —(1 hour later)— will be frequent. College work now demands the largest share of my time. Much of it is consumed in getting ready for classes. By that I mean seeing that materials are in hand and properly prepared for work. I have a couple of special students in the mornings from 9:30 to 12:30; a class in Pharmacy (Botany of course) from 10:30 to 12:30 on Tuesdays & Thursdays, elective Juniors 1:30—3:30 4 days per wk and Sophomores 1:30—3:30 2½ days per wk. College this year is unusually full. We have 90 Freshmen and 205 now enrolled in College, with 95 in Prep. Class. But I fear the "shop" is not interesting. — I have been carpentering during my spare moments in the mornings and evenings this week, — fixing up a summer kitchen or shed at the rear of the house so that it will be usable. In consequence my hands are all stiffened and "bunged up" generally. Wait till you move to an old house, with a landlord who isn't anxious to spend his money and you'll find out how many little things there are to be done to make life worth living! — All of which reminds me to ask how the vines

PURDUE UNIVERSITY,
LAFAYETTE, IND.

at the side of the house are coming on? Did our "fence" keep off the dogs while you were gone? And have those vines "caught on" yet? (Another break)

I ought to have acknowledged the receipt of your article on Hierochloa which has been forwarded to Coulter. It is quite interesting. I hope it will get out in Dec. We are now loaded up to the gunwales with A³S. stuff. Bailey is to have an article in Nov. with plate on hybrid Carices — one C. Knieskerni Dew. which has proved a puzzle heretofore. Beal also has a long paper on the Bulliform Cells in Grasses & Sedges with 2 plates. C. & A. are urgent that I begin my Fissidens paper in Nov. at latest and I may get it ready. Oct. no. we hope to get out once more on time. Sept. is delayed by A³S. material being late coming.

Kindest regards to Mrs. D.

Ever truly yours,

C. R. Barnes

Purdue University,
DEPARTMENT OF BIOLOGY.

LAFAYETTE, IND., Nov. 19. 1886.

My dear Deane:- I know you think me a scallawag and a rascal for not writing to you long ago. You will find out - if you are not already convinced of it, - that I am a great procrastinator and never do today what I can do tomorrow! My correspondents have been sending in mosses for me to determine and they have accumulated and the time has gone so fast that I fear the patience of the inquirers will be exhausted and my source of supply of mosses cut off - So I have been devoting my evenings - what few I can call my own - to studying the Bryums & Mniums and Hypnums and a host of other 'ums quite as knotty.

Then I have been indexing Vol. XI of the *Gazette*, so that your December number may not be delayed.

I have also been writing up my *Fissidens* revision which was to have commenced in the Nov. no. but was not ready and so must be postponed till Jan'y.

In addition I have to read a paper on Labor Organizations before the Parlor Club on Dec. 5, and as I don't know anything about the subject I have had to do a good deal of "grinding" for it.

Put my college work on top of that and you will see I am busy. Not too busy to write to you at all, but ~~too~~ busy enough to have a good excuse for deferring it.

Did I tell you that I had begun to get out a bundle of plants for you? I have —

but when it will be completed and ready to send I can't promise. I found that I have "stacks" of Sullivantia in flower but no fruit. I don't know that anything I can send will be of any account but I will send it some time and let you throw it away if you don't want it.

Bailey sent me the mosses he collected in Minn. last summer and Trelease sent the ones he picked up in the Rky Mts. Bailey writes that he is "busy". Have you his Carex set? His paper is quite a lucky one is n't it?

Doubtless you have gotten the back vols. of Gazette long ago. I wrote to Coulter at once on receipt of your letter and he said to you about them –

Coulter is coming up today at 2:30 to stay till midnight for a *Gazette* "Confab" –

I must close now and go over to the city to meet him –

With kindest remembrances to Mrs. G. and all Cambridge friends

Yours ever

C.R.Barnes

Has Mr. Watson gotten back yet? How does Kennedy come on? I am afraid he isn't going to forgive my neglect of him last summer – He's never answered my letter – May be he's paying me in my own coin!

–B

PURDUE UNIVERSITY.

LA FAYETTE, IND.

Purdue University,
DEPARTMENT OF BIOLOGY.

LAFAYETTE, IND., Dec. 15 1886.

My dear Deane:

Your letter came last week- Ever since then I have been driving on the year's index for the Gazette, which is now off hands-

Let me answer your questions first.

As to binding the Gazette- I should bind the 1st four volumes in one, the 5th & 6th in one, 7 & 8 in one, and 9 & 10 in one- A title page and index was issued with each two volumes I think- I kept my covers on. I should bind the general index as a separate thin volume, making the leaves flush with the cover-edges, which cover should be extra stiff-

I am afraid I have delayed answering your questions about the microscope too long-

I can get for you a microscope which will answer your every need for $36- The same instrument would probably cost you $45- A cheaper stand still is advertised by the Bausch & Lomb Opt. Co. (which I have not seen) at $40 and $32.50. These would cost me, $32 and $26 respectively. I am sure the latter would prove a most serviceable instrument from the known capability of the mfrs. If you want to get either of these I could send for one on approval and examine it before buying. You would never regret the putting of $26 into a microscope. Suppose you send for a Catalogue of microscopes to B. & L. Opt. Co., Rochester N.Y. and see cuts of 514 A, 513 B and 514 B for the low priced inst'm'ts and 521 for higher.

All goes on quietly here. I go to Indianapolis during the holidays to the meetings of Ind. Acad. Sci. and Ind. College Assn. Your Hierochloa paper is in Dec. Gaz. which will be delayed somewhat by index.

Kindest regards to Mrs. D. and yourself from us all.

Ever yours C. R. Barnes

Purdue University,
DEPARTMENT OF BIOLOGY.

LAFAYETTE, IND., Dec. 25 1886.

My dear Deane:–

Your kind remembrance came yesterday and I must thank you very much for your thoughtfulness and for the appropriate selection you made. I shall enjoy the Fresh fields I know, as I do all of Burroughs's writings–

I am writing to you with one of my Christmas presents under me — an office chair, revolving and adjustable for height — from mother– You know my fondness for all such conveniences and the et caeteras of a writer– I am a regular old granny about all such things– So I shall enjoy my chair and find it very useful I know. Perhaps you also know my weakness in [illegible] to cheese — do you? Well, my wife contributed to my comfort in extracting the article by giving me a cheese scoop. She said she felt somewhat as she imagined the man did who gave his wife a box of cigars! But I shall be the one to get the benefit of the cheese-scoop as she doesn't touch it.

My wife's father gave her an elegant mahogany music rack with mirror and shelf above for bric-a-brac. Her mother's present was as usual, money, from which she probably derives as much satisfaction as any thing else.

Ed fares well as usual. Seven books and playthings innumerable from his hosts of relations. Of all the things however, a train of cars, good, substantial iron ones, takes his eye and fills his heart. He has traveled about 6 miles with them already I think; round & round the room, under

Purdue University,
DEPARTMENT OF BIOLOGY.

LAFAYETTE, IND., 188

the table for his station and under my legs for a tunnel! Capacious tunnel, that!! —

One of my recent presents that I value highly is a Map of the U.S., 7 × 5½ mounted on cloth. This dated 1885 and published this last autumn by the Genl. Land Office. Write to your Congressman for one — You will value it I know — I have tacked mine to a spring curtain roller and put it up in my study.

I put on the backs of my Gazettes —

Botanical
Gazette

5 — 6 — this is the
1880 — 81 volumes

I should put extra stiff backs on the Index to make it stiff and bring the leaves flush with the edges because the pamphlet is so thin that you will find difficulty in opening unless you do so. The idea is to cut the backs and edges of the paper at the same time. You will find for this purpose paper sides the best I think. Of course if you wish to pay for it it can be bound like the rest and have the edges of the paper almost even with the binding nevertheless.

I wish I could dine with your company Monday. I should enjoy it immensely I know. Give my best wishes and kind regards to both your guests. With the compliments of the season to you and yours,

Sincerely as ever,

C. R. Barrett

The Botanical Gazette.

241 Columbia st.,
Jan. 8. 1886.

My dear Deane:—

I just write in haste to know if you will do me the favor of copying a couple of plates of ~~the~~ Bryologia Europaea for me?

I want from plate 363 (*Bryum bimum*) (1) the outline of the leaves of the various forms; (2) a section of the leaf showing how much the borders are revolute, and (3) the outline of the extreme forms (if more than one) of the capsule including the operculum—

From plate 176 (*Barbula rigidula* [Trichostomum]) I want a fig. of (1) the leaves in outline with a few cells drawn in from near the middle and a few [illegible] the base *if different*; (2) outline of Calyptra, operculum and capsule all in place if possible; if not, separate; (3) outline of a few teeth showing simply the width of membrane to which they are attached and how closely they are twisted.

Don't make your work too elaborate — the merest outlines will do.

Sincerely yours
C.R.B.

The Bryologia is in the Sullivant library & you'll have to ask Mr. Watson to get the 2 vols for you.

The Botanical Gazette.

EDITORS:

JOHN M. COULTER,
Wabash College, Crawfordsville, Ind.

CHARLES R. BARNES,
Purdue University, Lafayette, Ind.

J. C. ARTHUR,
Agric. Exper. Station, Geneva, N. Y.

241 Columbia st,
Jan. 13. 1887-

My dear Deane:-

In my hurried note to you last Saturday regarding the figures I wanted I did not take time to reply to your questions about the microscope-

Whenever you are ready send me word and I will order the instrument- I will order 521, ~~with a pair of steel forceps~~ - No, I remember I got you a pair of them - with the forceps omitted and an eye-shade (50¢) substituted- I should not advise you to get the alcohol lamp and cup there- Those fellows charge so much for such things- Instead of that write to Eimer and Amend, New York, for a 3 oz. alcohol lamp, No . of their Catalogue and a deep 2 or 2½ inch porcelain evaporating dish of the best make-

These will cost you about 50¢.-
You can then cut a Royal Baking Powder Can to make a support, or get your tinner at the square to make a wire tripod for you for a few cents. I don't believe you can buy an arrangement like Watson's-

Send me your order for the microscope when you are ready. I will then order it and have the bill sent to me. You can then send the money and I will pay it- Of course this arrangement will cost you something for the double expressage and remittance but you will save about $8 after all-

---

The fibro-vascular bundle of a herbaceous dicotyledon is bounded by parenchyma on all sides. Toward the center by pith parenchyma; toward the circumference by cortical parenchyma & on the sides by parenchyma which corresponds in position to the medullary rays but has no special name. The bundle in a woody dicot. is bounded on the inside by pith parenchyma, on the sides by medullary rays, and on the outside by the green layer of the bark = cortical parenchyma.

Pith	Wood		Bark		
Pith	Xylem (wood cells, tracheary tissue)	Cambium	Phloem (parenchyma, sieve cells, bast fibers)	Cort. par.	Epidermis or cork layer
Fundamental tissue	Bundle			Fundamental tissue	

Medullary Rays

The medullary rays belong to the fundamental system and the primary ones extend from the pith to the cortical parenchyma between the bundles. The secondary ones are shorter and do not reach the center. They lie between the newer bundles & are of various sizes according to age. In the above diagram the upper line shows the grouping and terms used in gross anatomy, the middle line the names of the tissues etc of histology and the lower line the grouping of these tissues. When a woody stem is young (say up to the end of the 1st season) it is covered by the epidermis which belongs to the epidermal system of tissues. When older this is suberised and sloughed off by the growth beneath it of cork which is developed from a special cork

of cortical parenchyma, transformed into a meristem tissue: hence the Cork belongs to the fundamental system –

All I have said applies to the stem bundles. In the root the bundle is single and axial, of the radial type, and bounded by (usually) a distinct sheath, which however is sometimes hardly distinguishable from the parenchyma which surrounds it –

Is that clear, mein Freund?

If so,
Auf wiederschreiben –
Barnes

Kind remembrances always to the Goodwife –

My dear Deane:-

Many thanks for the tracings which are very suitable for my use-

I ordered your microscope a day or two ago- I will send it unopened from here when it comes- I had them send the 521, with B Eyepiece, objectives 2/3 & 1/6 and Ward Eyeshade instead of pliers, slides & covers. The latter you can purchase at 6 Hamilton Place- I will let you know when to remit-

I write now chiefly to ask you to indicate on the pamphlet I send by this mail, the original paging in *Flora*, 1885 & 1886. You will find *Flora* at the Garden 1885, bound probably, and possibly 1886 bound, tho' the latter may be in the drawer or even at the binder's- Just pencil ~~on pages~~ the page of Flora and No. of volume on those pages only where a new installment begins. Take your time — no hurry — Yrs ever Barnes.

FROM
HAS. R. BARNES
LA FAYETTE, IND.

IF NOT CALLED FOR IN TEN DAYS, POSTMASTER WILL PLEASE RETURN TO

UNITED STATES
LETTER SHEET
ENVELOPE.

FAYETTE
JAN
4 PM

Walter Deane
Brewster Place
Cambridge,
Mass.

U. S. PATENT, JULY 1, 1879.

The Botanical Gazette.

EDITORS:

JOHN M. COULTER,
WABASH COLLEGE, CRAWFORDSVILLE, IND.

CHARLES R. BARNES,
PURDUE UNIVERSITY, LAFAYETTE, IND.

J. C. ARTHUR,
AGRIC. EXPER. STATION, GENEVA, N. Y.

January 27. 1887.

My dear Deane:-

Do not concern your righteous soul about the microscope not being good enough. Of course the costly ones are better — to a certain limit - but I assure you the Model is good enough for all practical purposes. I do not believe you will soon find any thing that you cannot observe satisfactorily with it. I think the talk about a condenser is all "guff" - Besides the Model will carry a condenser — when you think you want one $15 worth. I have worked a good deal at night and never found the need of one yet. In daylight one will not need one with anything less than 1000 — 1500 diameters — a power that a botanist (except bacteriologists) rarely has occasion to use. When you get able, buy a 1/8 and you will be amply equipped for all sorts of investigation, except bacteriology. The Model will carry any ob-

Now for your questions -

Sheet A.

1. The only reference on p. 74 that I find is in line 8 from bottom which refers to bast parenchyma. Bark consists of the inner bark (= the phloem region of the bundle which consists of phloem or bast parenchyma, sieve cells, and bast fibers); green layer (= cortical parenchyma); and outer layer (= cork) - "Bast" is loosely used to mean the whole phloem or only the bast fibers.

2. (a.) It is not necessary that as many segments should be cut off the outer side of the cambial cells as off the inner, nor is it the case. On the contrary the development of bast or phloem cells is much less rapid than the formation of xylem cells; hence the less thickness of the ~~bast part~~ (inner layer) of the bark.

(b.) The exfoliation of the bark frequently involves not only the outer layers but extends to the layers of phloem - E.g. the Grape does not develop much cork (if any) and the long strips of bark which peel off consist of bast fibers and phloem parenchyma - See p. 147. In many trees the formation of cork only occurs early and subsequently is sloughed off, i.e., when the "inner layer" has become thick enough to be protective - In other cases the cork development arises from a layer of bast parenchyma transformed into cork cambium. In the latter instance therefore it is a production of the technically "inner layer" of the bark. See p. 149.

3.(a) Does it not? (b) I don't know.

4.(a) I donot think it is very general but do not know. (b) I donot know.

Sheet B.

1. No. See Goodale, p. 149. In some cases it does however, when the cork is restricted to the outside and developed exclusively from the outer layer of cort.l parenchyma.

2. None whatever. The primary cortex early loses its chlorophyll as a rule.

3. Give it up! See 3 + 4 A, supra.

4. That is carrying things to extremes so to speak! I suppose they do. But who could distinguish a "primary" from a "secondary" bundle then?

5. The xylem (primary) lies at the central ends of the 4 medullary rays, the primary phloem at b. The lower + upper figures stand in the same relative position

6. See figure over. — This is a diagram of the young root ~~bu~~ cylinder of Phaseolus in the same relative position as in A + B. Prantl & Vines, p. 49. + corresponds to the shaded circle in A.

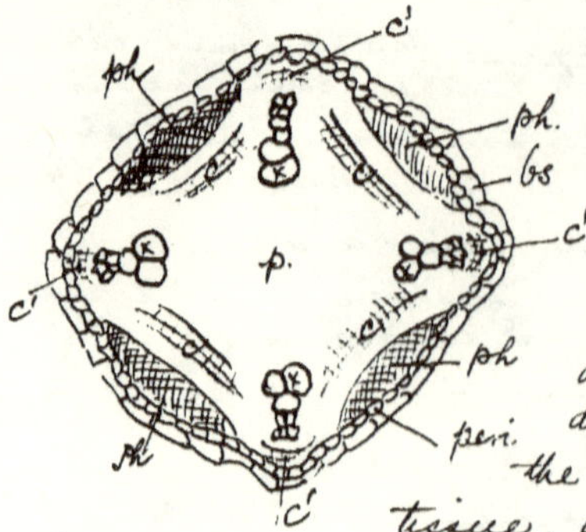

p = pith
peri = pericambium
ph = primary phloem
x = primary xylem
c, c' = cambium
b.s = bundle sheath.

In the young roots this bundle cylinder is differentiated from the fundamental tissue, a short distance from the root-tip. Secondary changes begin by the transformation of the parenchyma cells in the regions c & c' into cambium. c, c, c, c give rise on the inner side (by the differentiation of their [illegible]) to <u>secondary xylem</u> which finally results in the 4-armed cross shaded darkest in B. On its outer side this cambium produces secondary bast, represented in fig B. by the dark clusters of cells surrounding the xylem cross, (b' b') but not coalescing with the primary phloem b, b. The cambium in the regions c', c', c', c', does not produce either xylem or phloem but only horizontally elongated parenchyma cells which separate the xylem into the 4 parts. c & c' are of course continuous but I have left them separate in the figure I drew to let you locate them better.

At K fig B, outside both primary & secondary phloem the cells have produced a cork cambium. Thus the secondary structure of the root comes to resemble closely that of the stem, though originally very different.

See Goodale p. 112. In that figure C is the tissue on each side the xylem which gives rise to cambium which in turn produces secondary xylem & phloem. Thus the secondary xyl. alternates with the primary, whereas the secondary phloem is opposed to the primary.

Verstehen Sie?

7. The cork cannot be included in the term "primary cortex" which is applied only to the fundamental tissue developed from the primary meristem at the apex. Prantl & Vines do not mean it so. Vide fig. 63 p. 62.

8. Yes. The primary cortex does not always last through the life of a tree. In some cases it is sloughed off quite early. See A. 2. b. supra.

you for and shall hereafter call for—

When you have $7^{00} ~~to spare~~ buy Sachs 2nd Ed. You will find it very useful when y'r microscope comes—

Yours ever
C. R. Barnes

My wife has been confined to her bed for a week past but is now sitting up— Hope Mrs. D's cold will be easily gotten rid of— Kindest regards to her—

You make my mouth water when you relate ~~your~~ the recent encounter ~~with~~ between the Kennedy dinner and a Blue Hill appetite!

B.

(1) Goodale on p. 74, speaks of "Bast, in the inner bark." Strictly speaking, is not the Bast the phloem of the fibro-vascular bundle?

(2) If the cambium, in the open bundles of exogens, makes Bast on one side, wood on the other, why in a tree is there so little bast compared to the wood? The Bast being crowded [illegible]

(3) Why does not the Phelloderm, in plants which have it, increase in thickness? It is internal. In such plants is the phelloderm produced yearly by the cork cambium?

4) Do most plants have Phelloderm (in exogens) and does it last with the age of the plant?

A.

Return this -

B–

Return –

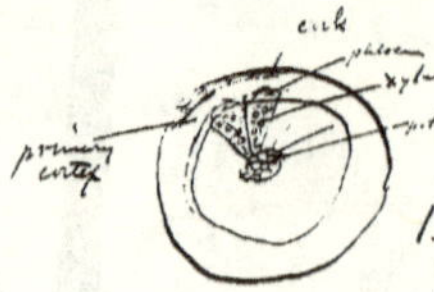

Stem say 4 yrs. old. I examined one like this –

1. As this grows into a large limb or trunk, does not the primary cortex always remain permanent as a thin layer between the periderm (cork) and the phloem (bast)?

2. When the phelloderm (a green layer) is made by the phellogen (cork cambium) ~~[illegible]~~ it has no reference to the primary cortex, has it?

3. How often is phelloderm made and does it last through the age of the tree? It is not made every year, is it? If so, would not the periderm increase much in thickness?

4. Do not the extreme outside of the phloem and inside of the xylem belong to the primary bundle, I mean in an old exogenous stem?

5. Will you explain the position of the xylem & phloem (in Prantl & Vines page 49) in the section of the older root. They should be radial. 6. I don't understand the secondary bast. How does the root increase in growth?

7. In an old trunk (exogen) would you use the term "primary cortex" as applied to the cork? Prantl & Vines say it is all that is external to the bast (p 54).

ĩmes! This resembles a previous questi

Purdue University,
DEPARTMENT OF BIOLOGY.

LAFAYETTE, IND., Jan. 29 1887.

My dear Deane:—

I reshipped to you today the box with Microscope per Am. Exp.— Charges from Rochester here and here to Camb. Collect—

Bill enclosed. Please remit and return bill to me— I will pay B of L and send you receipt.

Yrs in haste

Barnes

The Botanical Gazette.

EDITORS.

JOHN M. COULTER,
WABASH COLLEGE, CRAWFORDSVILLE, IND.

CHARLES R. BARNES,
PURDUE UNIVERSITY, LAFAYETTE, IND.

J. C. ARTHUR,
AGRIC. EXPER. STATION, GENEVA, N. Y.

Feb. 12/87

Dear Deane:- Glad to know the Kennedys are safe - It was a close shave - Was the train running in two sections or were they on an earlier one?

Will it be asking too much to ask you to copy for me the Key to species from Braithwaite's Sphagnaceae? You will find it among the B's in the 2nd alcove from the Herb. door and about the 2nd shelf

Laf. 2/5/87-

Dear Deane:- Do let me hear at once whether Kennedy was on the illfated Vermont Centl. train for Montreal! I have a letter dated Feb. 3 which says he expects to leave on the 4th- I am very anxious.

Yrs ever Barnes—

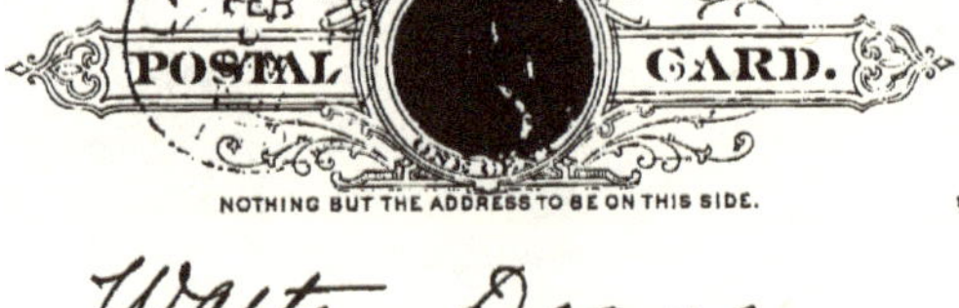

NOTHING BUT THE ADDRESS TO BE ON THIS SIDE.

Walter Deane
Cambridge
Brewster Pl. Mass.

The Botanical Gazette.

EDITORS.
JOHN M. COULTER, Wabash College, Crawfordsville, Ind.
CHARLES R. BARNES, Purdue University, Lafayette, Ind.
J. C. ARTHUR, Agric. Exper. Station, Geneva, N. Y.

February 7. 1887 -

My dear Deane:-

About your microscope - Did the book come with it? - The B eyepiece & 1/4 obj. give only 250 diameters - It seems I have been estimating all the time on the C. which is the one that we have with ours - A & C. Instead of buying another objective I should advise you to get a D eyepiece which will cost you only $4 or perhaps I can get it for $3 - In case you want a condenser you can get a substage adapter for $1.00 and use your 1 in objective, which answers admirably -

As to systematic work - Why not use our handbook and commence on the Capsella? I can send you material for histological work by mail or express -

Replying to your questions.

1. A binary root is one having a double mass of xylem in the central f-v. cylinder, so arranged as to form a plate of tissue dividing the cylinder into 2 parts. The xylem plate extends diametrically from pericambium to pericambium. See Goodale figs. 93, 94, 95.

2. Bundle sheath = Endodermis. The pericambium is the layer of cells just inside this from which in Phanerogams new branches of the roots arise — "Peripheral layer" I presume means the cortex of the root, viz: all outside the axial cylinder. You will have to be guided by context as the term is not a special one.

3. I suppose not though I am not informed as to this special case. I presume the cambium simply arises from pericambial cells instead of from the parenchyma of the axial cylinder —

4. Yes; so long at least as new roots (i.e., branches) are being produced – How much longer I do not know –

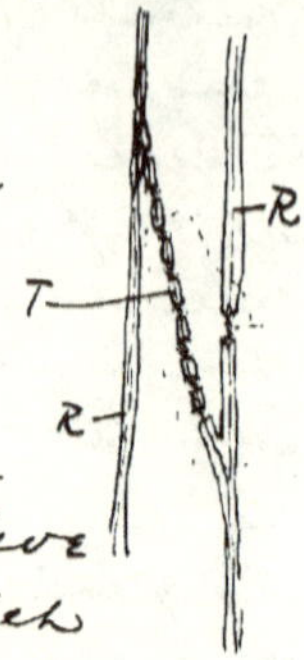

5. Goodale fig. 75.

The sketch at the side shows more of the same figure. The portion included by dotted line shows the part Goodale figures – RR = radial walls of a sieve cells (i.e., those walls which are parallel to radii drawn from center of stem. In fig. 74 the two walls with sieve plates on them are radial walls) T = terminal partition (i.e., the end wall of one sieve cell.)

CC = callus, covering & closing the pores of the sieve plate –

In the explanation of fig. 75 change 6th word "tube" to plate – i.e., sieve plate – "Tube" a lapsus pennae.

p. 113 § 343 1st paragraph – The roots of most monocotyledons remain small and hence the axial cylinder...

does not undergo the secondary changes — i.e., the formation of a cambium layer and the production from this of rings of wood and bark. But in the tree-like Monocots (Dracaena [and Palms?]) these changes do occur in order to produce the large roots necessary.

I see I've taken the wrong section, but I can't afford to throw away this sheet, so cross it out.

Understand by "level of the root" distance from the growing tip, and it will be clear, will it not? —

Yours sincerely
C. R. Barnes

2. Distinguish bundle sheath, pericambium & endodermis. & periphyseal layer —

3. You showed me how in a root the cambium forms making a continuous ring inside the the primary phloem and outside the primary xylem. Goodale on p. 113 § 346 speaks of wood & liber being formed by the pericambium in some cases. Does that mean that both these cambiums are working at the same time?

4. Does the pericambium always for a certain length of time continue active?

5. I dont understand in Goodale p. 93. fig 75 nor p. 113 § 345 1st paragraph.

The Botanical Gazette.

EDITORS:

241 Columbia st.,
February 16. 1889.

My dear Deane:-

Do not be afraid to "impose on my kindness"! You will find that I manage to repay myself by demands on your time in the way of looking up references etc at the Garden!

Shall I send for the set of slides gotten up to illustrate Bessey's botany and look them over? I have no doubt B. & L. will send them to me on approval and take them back if I do not think them good. Are you ready to put the money into such a set? I will defer ordering the D eyepiece until I hear about this, so as to get both together.

The only way to make sections is — to make them, and keep on until you gain skill. Send to J. R. Torrey Mfg. Co. Worcester, Mass. for their razor ground flat on lower side when held in right hand, edge toward you. Get this, if you are needing to buy a new razor. If you have a suitable one you can get along without this. See Handbook for directions.

Goodale p. 113 § 342 and 343, is undoubtedly not lucid. Here's what I make out of a careful study of it.

"In the cortex, according to Olivier, the secondary tissues are either parenchymatous or suberous.

"The secondary parenchyma of the [cortex] proceeds from the [pericambium] of the central cylinder.

"The cortical parenchyma is renewed ~~by layers of cells just outside the~~ by [the internal ~~layer~~ zone of the cortex] (see e fig. 93).

[Reconcile those two statements if you can: I can't & have written to Goodale about it.]

"The suberous tissue in gymnosperms and in dicotyledons with caducous primary cortex is derived from the pericambium x x x In the case of woody dicots xxx and in monocots it is produced in the external zone of the cortical parenchyma x x x

"343. In a given species, the [distance from the tip of the root at which the secondary changes begin to take place ~~from~~ by which cork or suberous tissue is produced] depends on the transverse diameter of the root, x x x" [Below that point the primary structure of the root is unchanged. The point at which these secondary tissues appear advances pari passu with the tip of the root.]

Remember that the primary tissues are those differentiated from the primary meristem and secondary tissues are those arising from any ~~other~~ one of these primary tissues by their conversion into a secondary meristem or their persistence in a meristematic condition, resuming activity after a time—

Does this clear it up any? If not ask again and I'll try again—

Yours ever,

C.R. Barnes

"Peripheral layer" = pericambium
"Cortical parenchyma = either primary or secondary parenchyma of the cortex. May be either cork or parenchyma in the secondary cortex; or both.

I find that I do not understand Goodale, p 113 - §§ 342-343 - In figures 93-94-95 he calls the cylinder inside the endodermis a bundle sheath, the peripheral layer. You say the pericambium is just within the bundle-sheath. It would seem from that that they were synonymous. But Goodale in § 342 speaks of the peripheral layer & pericambial layer as two distinct things - It would seem that the latter were outside the former. Your explanation of the increase in a root was in the central cylinder. What I want is a short explanation of the increase in the cortex. What is the difference between secondary & cortical parenchyma? There seems to be a cambium for both and one for the suberous tissue. Is that so? Do all roots have cork & parenchyma in the cortex? I still don't understand 343 -

Extract from Goodale's letter to Barnes about § 343 in Goodale's Botany

"The last quotation beginning 'The cortical parenchyma is renewed' should be preceded by the words, - according to Van Tieghem, on the other hand &c. The previous paragraphs are substantially Olivier's views, as shown by the citation" Feb. 24 - 1887

March 11th 1887.

My dear Deane:–

Yes, sir, I got your letter of Feb. 20 and it is a shame that I did not answer it promptly but since that time I've just been on the keen jump! I have not yet ordered your D Eye-piece but will do so by this mail, and will also ask B & L to send me the slides on approval–

I will willingly examine a transverse section of Aristolochia if you will send me a piece in alcohol– The piece you sent was of course shrivelled when it reached me– You will find alcoholic material far superior to fresh *for sections*. I will send you the section to.

Goodale's reply was — as usual — very unsatisfactory. I enclose it. Please return.

"With Late-formed secondary vessels" are simply includes those plants whose secondary vessels do not develop early.

I have been constructing a recording auxanometer of the most approved pattern. This well on the way, and I hope to complete it tomorrow. The cylinder is of ash, with central steel axis, resting in a glass cup below, and rotated by a weight. The lower end of the cylinder has 24 pegs equidistant. A stop which catches on each of these pegs is drawn away by an electro-magnet which acts every hour, the circuit being closed by the striking arm of a clock. This allows the cylinder to make 1/24 of a revolution. A pen supported on the thread from the plant bears against the paper on the cylinder & makes an ink tracing like this: in

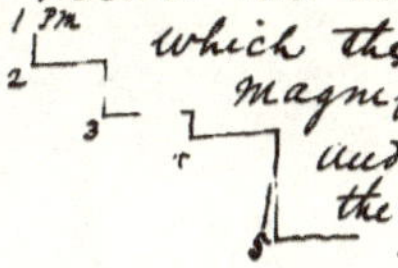

which the vertical element is the magnified growth of the plant and the horizontal element the 1/24 revolution of the cylinder each hour. Sabe?

Dear Deane:— Can you find out for me whether the "New England Decorative Work. #19 Pearl St." is a reliable house?

Yours Ever

Barnes

POSTAL CARD.

UNITED STATES ONE CENT

MAR 16 1 AM 1887

NOTHING BUT THE ADDRESS TO BE ON THIS SIDE.

Walter Deane
Cambridge
Mass.

3/21/87—

Dear D: I send Eyepiece today. Billed @ $3.00 The slides they will send to me shortly— More anon—

Yrs ever

B

UNITED STATES

POSTAL CARD.

ONE CENT

NOTHING BUT THE ADDRESS TO BE ON THIS SIDE.

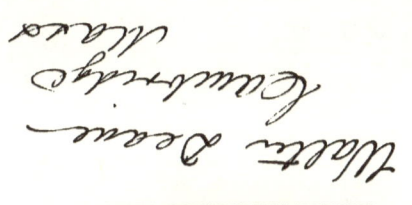

Walter Deane
Cambridge
Mass

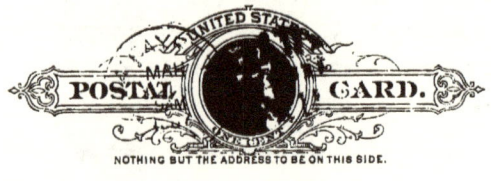

The Botanical Gazette.

EDITORS:

JOHN M. COULTER,
WABASH COLLEGE, CRAWFORDSVILLE, IND.

CHARLES R. BARNES,
PURDUE UNIVERSITY, LAFAYETTE, IND.

J. C. ARTHUR,
AGRIC. EXPER. STATION, GENEVA, N. Y.

Sunday, Apr. 3. 1887.

My dear Deane:-

By a mere chance I got your letter today instead of on Monday and I write at once to say that you must stop with us when you come to Chicago. I suppose you are going to visit your brother and his wife there. Now you can give us at least a couple of days at the end of Easter week and get back to your school in time. I shall take it as a personal affront if you don't come!

My wife joins me in urging you to stop. She says she wants to have an opportunity of showing you some kindness in recognition of that you showed me when a "lone wanderer".-

Do Come. I want so much to see you and talk with you again.

Does Mrs. D. come with you? I hope she does. We would be so glad to welcome you both. Let me hear from Cambridge or Chicago. And don't dare to say you won't stop—

Auf wiedersehen — I hope —

C. R. Barnes

April 9. 1887.

My dear Deane:—

I am going now to give you a full and complete answer to all your recent letters, all of which I have enjoyed getting but have been too "rushed" for a little season to answer.

<u>To the letter of Mch. 13th.</u>

Did I then not even acknowledge the receipt of your copying? What a careless wretch! Yes, I got it in good time and used it to good advantage in constructing a key to the N. Am. Sphagnaceae. Did I tell you that I was making Keys to all the large genera? It's a pretty tough job sometimes. I could not depend upon the Braithwaite Key, as it combines several species (properly enough) which L. & J. recognize as

Cambridge and begin work on a Moss Flora which would be more to my liking that the present one.

Watson said a good word for my Fissidens work and expressed the hope that I would continue it.

March 14th 1887.

At present I have no students working on histological work. My Juniors (elective) are doing experimental work in physiology and the Freshmen are on structural work (gross) in Phanerogams. The Sophomores I have only the first half year. It is rare that a student gets a section worth saving. When it happens I always keep it and add it to our slide collection. I wrote to B. & L. about the set of slides & they said they hoped to be able to send one shortly. This has not been done however.

Good sections are rarely whole, and fragmentary ones as a rule are best for a close study of the cells. When one wants to get the tout ensemble (so to speak) he has to resort to thick entire sections. This is the reason why "boughten" slides are rarely worth having. The "microscopist" is not pleased with the looks of a fragmentary section and in order to make a pretty slide he has to use thick sections.

The Aristolochia which you promise in this letter came yesterday. I am mounting a section of it & will send it you shortly, with an explanation. Caution: when you put histological material into alcohol to preserve it, immerse at first in at least 10 times its bulk of alcohol. Afterwards (2 or 3 days) it may be placed in a bottle with just enough to cover it and will keep indefinitely.

You will find Strasburger's Practical Botany (a translation by Hillhouse of Strasburger's "Das kleine botanische Practicum") just out, a most helpful book in the line of study you are beginning.

Copy <u>by all means</u>.

My auxanometer is a daisy! It works like a charm. The tracings are very clear and instructive. Did I explain the mechanism to you? Here it is in a nutshell:—

C is a wooden cylinder, which revolves upon a brass spindle resting on

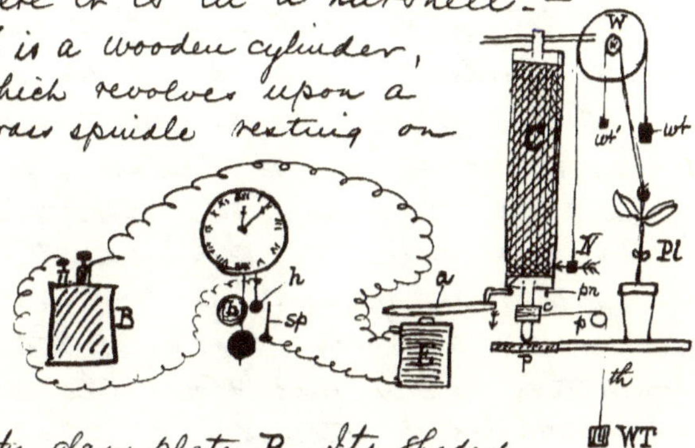

the glass plate, P. Its shaded part is covered with paper and smoked over a turpentine flame. c is a spool around which passes a thread, th, over the pulley <u>p</u>, from the weight <u>WT</u>. This drives the cylinder, which would therefore rotate continuously but for the series of 13 pins <u>pn</u> around its circumference, [there are 13 because the old clock wheel which I fastened to the lower end of the cyl. <u>had</u> 13 pins in it. I wanted <u>12</u>.] which engage with an armature a, of an Electro-magnet, E. In the circuit of a Leclanché battery B is placed a clock arranged, by fastening the striking wheel, to strike but once each hour. When, at the hour, the hammer h draws back to strike the bell b it touches the spring sp and for an instant closes the circuit. E becomes a magnet, pulls down the armature a, which releases the cylinder. But before the next pin comes around the circuit has been broken, the armature rises and stops the cylinder. A thread attached to the upper end of an internode of a plant Pl. passes over a small wheel w attached to the same spindle as a larger wheel W, 10 times the diameter of the smaller. This thread is kept taut but a light weight wt. Over the larger wheel goes a thread one end of which carries a weight with a needle N passing through it and the other end a counterpoise weight wt. Any upward growth of the plant moves the wheel W and consequently the needle N, 10 times as far. The needle scratches off the soot and leaves a white mark. Growth marks are vertical: movements of cylinder cause horizontal mark.

I send you by this mail, to Cambridge, another copy of my Key.

Here is a sketch of a leaf of Fissidens rufulus.

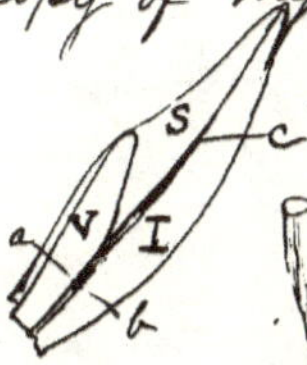

Fig. 1.

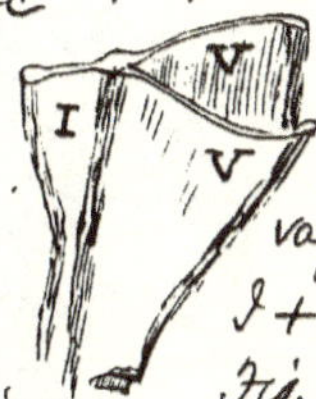

Fig. 2

I is the inferior lamina, S = superior lamina, V = vaginant lamina. I + S = vertical lamina. Fig. 2 is the part of Fig. 1 below ab. V is double, sheathing the stem and S & I are vertical in position. C is the Costa.

March 20. 1887.

How I should have liked to be at that dinner party. Truly it was select. Tell me more about Gray's new book if you know. I am at the first of it.

The questions enclosed in this letter are answered on the same sheet which is enclosed herein.

I have just gotten your last letter saying that you were not coming. I am very sorry you could not find time, but I know how you will find the time fly. Some other time I shall claim a special visit.

There is little of news to write. Ed has been sick for a couple of weeks with a low fever — Just sick enough to be cross and not enough to be dangerously ill. Mother went this morning to Piqua Ohio to visit her sister for a week. I keep in excellent health and am busy all the time. My wife has not been well but is better now. [She has met her woman's fate again.]

Write soon and tell me about your Chicago visit —

Kind regards to Mrs Deane from all of us and Easter greetings —

Yours Ever, C.P. Brown

Gray's Bot. Text-Book. Answered
Vol II. Ap. 7, 8?

Phys. Botany — Goodale.

(1) Page 173. Figure c  I don't understand the arrangement of bundles. I presume a, a, a, are the bundles of the dorsal suture. b and the two corresponding ones of the ventral or are the ventral ones the little one I have not figured? Where are the other ones I have not lettered?

---

a, a, a = f.v.b's of dorsal suture
The f.v.b's of ventral suture are the small pairs not figured above but shown in the original —
b, b, and the rest are blended (or in the lower side separate) bundles of the carpels, thus:

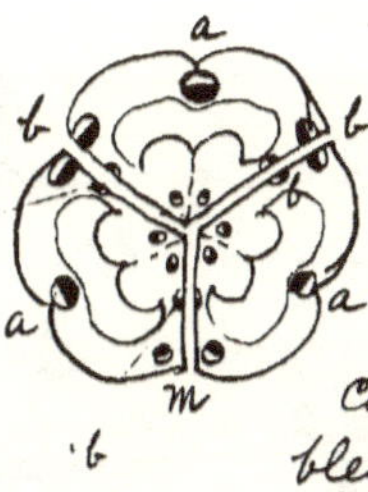

Dotted line = line of union of carpels.

Here the carpels are slightly separated but in the same position as above —
aaa = dorsal f.v.b's.
bbbbb = bundles of contiguous carpels which blend —
m = a pair which do not blend.
The six small ones at center are ventral f.v.b's

(2) Page 175 - Fig. a. I don't see how how the 3 bundles described as dorsal ones can be from their position -

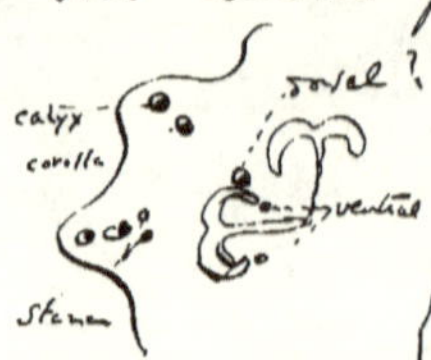

From that position I can't follow the line of the carpellary leaf - I have always considered the dorsal suture thus:-

"This would seem to correspond to the dorsal suture in Van Tieghem's fig. above.

I can't explain this - Either I'm very stupid or "some one has blundered" - <u>Ask Goodale</u>, & let me know what he says -

I have the same trouble with Fig. b - p. 174.

(3) Figs on Page 181 - Why is a in fig. 138. fruit-capsule and in the others chaff? Where are the two integuments to the seed and is 'c' an inner integument?

Because (I suppose) the sections of the latter grains (whose chaff is adherent) were cut through chaff and all - I am not sure of the homology of <u>c</u> but think it equivalent to <u>perisperm</u> - It can hardly be inner integument -

The Botanical Gazette.

EDITORS:

JOHN M. COULTER,
WABASH COLLEGE, CRAWFORDSVILLE, IND.

CHARLES R. BARNES,
PURDUE UNIVERSITY, LAFAYETTE, IND.

J. C. ARTHUR,
AGRIC. EXPER. STATION, GENEVA, N. Y.

April 19 –

Dear Deane:– I write you but a word – That is one that wrings my heart.

Our Eddie lies at the point of death with cerebral meningitis and we have no hope of his recovery. Since last Wednesday evening

We called the most skillful physicians in the State but he is beyond the skill of man — and has been for weeks, tho' he became alarmingly sick only last Wednesday.

Looking back over his life we can see how ~~the~~ disease has approached so insidiously that none could have recognized its coming —

Oh it's so hard to give him up —

Yours ever

C. R. B.

The Botanical Gazette.

April 20. 1887.

My dear Deane:—

The worst that we feared has come.—

Eddie died quietly at five o'clock this morning.—

We shall bury him on Friday at 3 P.M.—

Yours, in sorrow,

C. R. Barnes

Lafayette, Ind.
May 24. 1887.

My dear Deane:–

I know you are out of all patience with me because I have been so long in writing to you. But it did not seem to me for a few weeks that I could write and tell you about our great loss. My work too had got in arrears and that gave me opportunity to persuade myself that I did not have time – Really I was and have been up to the present moment very busy: but I think the real reason that I did not write was that necessity of telling of Eddie's sickness. I do not allow myself to think of it if I can help it and I keep over head and ears ~~in~~ work so that I may not. Of course it all comes over me now and then and I realize that he is gone — and I feel as though I could not bear it — ——— — Mary tells me that she wrote to your wife a day or two ago — After all women are braver than men. — I send you by this mail Eddie's picture —

Long ago I prepared sections of the Aristolochia and had them all ready to send. But some one laid a box down on the slide and destroyed it. I recently made some more. The slide is not so well mounted as the first one, but shows better the stem structure. There seems to be little to explain. The central pith has some empty and some starch-filled cells. Next the pith the tips of the fibro-vascular bundles have spiral vessels, slightly thicker-walled than the adjoining wood-cells and the large vessels (pitted) which compose the bulk of the xylem. The cambium extends between the xylem and phloem and stretches from one bundle to the next. These parts are the interfascicular cambium from which the medullary ray tissue arises. The phloem consists chiefly of parenchyma containing starch I cannot surely distinguish the sieve cells in transverse section but suppose they are those cells with strongly refringent contents here and there. It is not unlikely that some of the cells with shrunken contents may be also sieve cells. Make a longitudinal section and you can determine. Bounding the phloem is an indistinct bundle sheath, the cells elongated circumferentially. Outside the phloem lies

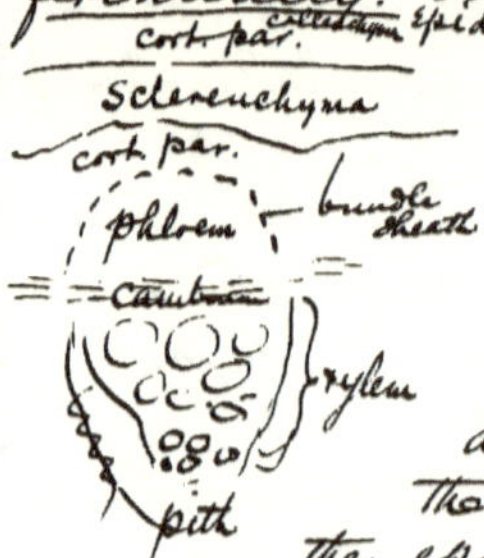

the cortical parenchyma, separated into 2 zones by a zone of sclerenchyma fibers. Outside the cortical parenchyma, making about 1/2 the space from the sclerenchyma zone to the epidermis is collenchyma. The epidermis has a very thick outer wall with a distinct cuticle. If you can't make all this out I will answer any special questions. You will find a section of the stem taken now (this year's shoots) more instructive than the year-old ones.

~~Saturday~~ I got back from Waveland where the Indiana Academy of Science held its spring (field) meeting. There were about thirty in attendance and we had a jolly time. We visited the "Shades of Death" and "Pine Hills", two romantic places near Waveland, and about 50 miles from here. On Thursday and Friday we ~~took~~ luncheon in the woods and spent the days collecting. I got about 20 species of mosses which is a large find for two days.

I have under consideration a change in location. The State University at Bloomington ~~are~~ is asking me to take the botanical chair. I don't know how the matter will come out. It is to be decided early in June.

I will write again soon. I have been so interrupted and bothered by talking in this letter that I have forgotten about all I was going to tell you. Yours ever C. R. Barnes.

The Botanical Gazette.

EDITORS:

JOHN M. COULTER,
WABASH COLLEGE, CRAWFORDSVILLE, IND.

CHARLES R. BARNES,
PURDUE UNIVERSITY, LAFAYETTE, IND.

J. C. ARTHUR,
AGRIC. EXPER. STATION, GENEVA, N. Y.

241 Columbia st.,
June 25. 1887.

My dear Deane:—

Well, my fate is sealed! I have just accepted the Professorship of Botany in the Univ. of Wisconsin, which Sargent owing to a complete break-down in his health had to resign. It came about in this way.

A couple of weeks ago I had a letter from Chamberlin the Pres.-elect asking whether I would consider an offer from them, and stating the condition and prospects of the University. I replied that I would be inclined to consider it favorably and would come to Madison to look over the ground if they made me an offer. He said so. I therefore left for Madison on Sunday night at two o'clock and reached M. the next afternoon at 2:30, staying till Wednesday night, through their Commencement exercises.

The state of affairs is about this: Madison is situated on several low hills between lakes Mendota and Monona. Mendota lake is about 8 x 6 miles and Monona about half the size. The town is a beautiful one; clean, wellkept lawns, no fences and pretty houses. The capitol stands in a park of 14 acres surrounded by trees. Westward runs State st. to the College campus a mile away on another hill. The view from the college is strikingly like a look up Pennsylvania ave. towards the Capitol from the White House. The capitol dome is modeled after the one at Washington which adds to the resemblance. Madison has about 15,000 inhabitants.

The University grounds ...

The Botanical Gazette.

EDITORS:

JOHN M. COULTER, Wabash College, Crawfordsville, Ind.

CHARLES R. BARNES, Purdue University, Lafayette, Ind.

J. C. ARTHUR, Agr. Exp. Station, Geneva, N. Y.

about 200 acres of rolling land, partly in trees and partly in lawn and partly in experimental plats. "Mendota Drive" winds through the grounds and along the lake's edge and is said to be ~~about~~ several miles long. The site is the most beautiful one for college buildings I have ever seen.

The buildings are, Library Hall (Library & Chapel) University Hall (the oldest) Agricultural Hall, North Hall, Ladies Dormitory, Chemical Laboratory, Mechanic Shop, ~~and~~ Science Hall, Washburn Observatory and a Students' Observatory. The Students' observatory has a small telescope of 6 in. aperture and other instruments for their unrestricted use. The Washburn observatory is admirably equipped. The main telescope is 13.5 in. aperture and stands next to the Cambridge instrument. There are also other instruments of the best quality.

Science Hall is not quite complete

complete. We expect to get into it next January tho' the architect promises it by Sept. I am to have the third floor with the Zoologist. The building is of pressed brick, 3 stories and high basement and is completely fire-proof. Its interior is to be on the same general sty[le] as the new wing of Agassiz Museum, except that the walls are finished in tile instead of plaster. The outside is very much more ornate. It will cost about $250,000. The plan of the 3rd floor is like this:

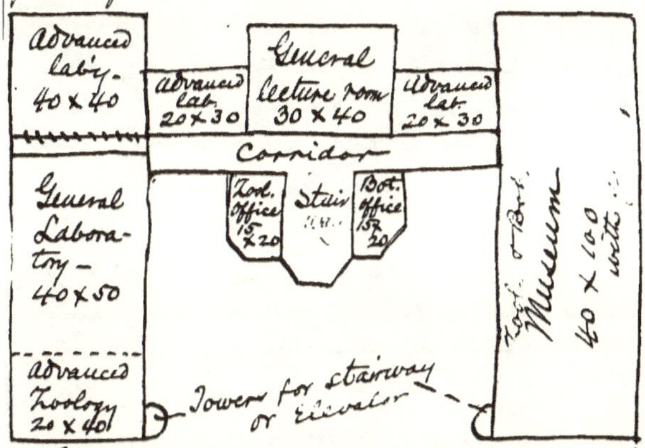

The sizes are only guess work tho' I stepped some of the rooms. The apportionment of rooms is not

The Botanical Gazette.

entirely decided on yet but it will be somewhat as indicated. The second floor is occupied by Dep't of Geology and Metallurgy, first by Physics and Mech. Engineering, basement by various things. The Chem. Lab. is of Milwaukee brick, very plain outside but elaborate inside and completely equipped. A boiler house near by furnishes steam to Mech. Shops, Chem. Lab. and Science Hall.

The Legislature is liberal towards the institution and the people are proud of it. The Univ. consists of a College of Arts offering a course in General Science and special technical courses in Agriculture, Pharmacy, Civil Engineering, Mining Eng., Metallurgical Eng. and Mechanical Engineering; the College of Letters, offering courses in Ancient Classics, Modern Classics and English; and a College of Law.

An appropriation of $12,000 annually

for holding farmer's institutes over the state, is controlled by the Univ. —— But I'll not weary you further. The outlook seems to me good; hence I go.

I spent the week after our Commencement at Hanover, my alma mater, renewing the acquaintances and reviving the memories of 10 years ago. — Had a very pleasant visit.

Can you tell me whether the Concord School of Philosophy publishes its Proceedings and Lectures and if so where the volume can be obtained?

Write to me and tell me your plans for the summer. We shall not move till 1st of Sept.

My wife sends kindest regards to you both. Mother is away on a visit —

Ever truly yours,

C.R. Barnes

The Botanical Gazette.

EDITORS:

JOHN M. COULTER,
WABASH COLLEGE, CRAWFORDSVILLE, IND.

CHARLES R. BARNES,
PURDUE UNIVERSITY, LAFAYETTE, IND.

J. C. ARTHUR,
AGRIC. EXPER. STATION, GENEVA, N. Y.

241 Columbia st.,
Aug. 8. 1887.

My dear Denne:-

Some time ago, you may remember, I wrote you that I was getting out a package of plants for you. From the time that elapsed without your hearing any further from them you probably concluded that they were mythical. I don't remember what put a stop to my going over the duplicates — something did — and now a full stop is put to it by my going to Madison. I therefore send you what I had picked out, 18 species, most of which you will probably not care for. Only Leavenworthia, ~~Sullivantia~~ Sullivan-tia and Schizaea are of much account, though Asplenium pinnatifidum is not abundant. Use what you want and throw the rest away. The plants have all been poisoned but the Schizaea and I see no sign of bugs, but you will want to soak them well I know, before they go in with the "elect." I send the package to Cambridge with the request not to forward, lest they may share the fate of a photo which I sent you to Nantucket a couple of weeks ago. Evidently it had not arrived when you wrote. Did you leave your address with the P.M. on Nantucket? Maybe it will get to you yet.

I enclose the labels, so you can see what the package contains though you may not feast your eyes on the charming (?) specimens until your home-coming.

I begin the pleasant (?) business of packing tomorrow. It will be an interminable job I fear.

The Botanical Gazette.
EDITORS:
JOHN M. COULTER, WABASH COLLEGE, CRAWFORDSVILLE, IND.
CHARLES R. BARNES, PURDUE UNIVERSITY, LAFAYETTE, IND.
J. C. ARTHUR, AGRIC. EXPER. STATION, GENEVA, N. Y.

One doesn't know how many pictures, vases et id omne genus one has until he comes to pack them separately for transportation. I shall begin with the bric-a-brac and dishes (except the ones in daily use) and then take the books and my special plunder. Furniture we will have packed by an expert — there's the good of marrying a furniture store! — and therefore I shall leave that out of the count. Matters are complicated by the necessity of my being at Madison about Sept. 1, and the necessity of my wife's being here for a month or so longer. We've about concluded to pack everything but the necessaries for two rooms and kitchen and let Mary and Mother keep the establishment here until M. can travel, which we expect will be by the last week in September. Did you know that the Treleases have a boy, born June 28? "Mother and Child doing well" Trelease writes me under date of Aug. 4.

Knowlton is out in the Nat'l Park with Ward, collecting fossil and living plants. He is to get what mosses he can for me. They will be gone until Oct. 1. I suppose Underwood is off somewhere as I can't stir him up. Arthur, (J.C., of the N.Y. Agric. Exp. Sta.) is to be my successor here, until the Hatch Bill appropriation is passed by Congress, when he is to take charge of the experiment station in botany. That will bring Stanley Coulter (bro. of John) to the place of Prof. of Botany.

I suppose you'll never go to the A.A.A.S. now! You let the Buffalo meeting slip through your fingers and now the New York

The Botanical Gazette.
EDITORS:
JOHN M. COULTER, WABASH COLLEGE, CRAWFORDSVILLE, IND.
CHARLES R. BARNES, PURDUE UNIVERSITY, LAFAYETTE, IND.
J. C. ARTHUR, AGRIC. EXPER. STATION, GENEVA, N. Y.

meeting goes by right under your nose and I don't hear a chirp about your attending! Why don't you go and get acquainted with the botanists?

I have been putting in my best licks for a few weeks on determining some collections of mosses – I still have a large number of my own collecting and from Idaho (up at Pend' Oreille lake) to determine – They keep coming. I've more correspondents in this country than I can keep up with and there are several I've promised in Europe –

The inquiry about the Proceedings of the Concord School of Philosophy were made for a friend, who will be very glad to know where the volumes can be obtained – Thank you for the information and the kind offer of the 1885 vol.

Wish we had been having the superfluous part of your "lots of rain" - Everything in this part of the country is parched and the corn crop is nearly ruined - There has not a drop of rain fallen on Lafayette since July 4! and only a hard shower then.

Bausch & Lomb have never "Chirped" about the slides after that letter I sent you - Shall I do anything further?

Kindest regards to Mrs. Deane from us all -

Ever sincerely yours,

C. R. Barnes

Please address me
hereafter at
Madison, Wisc.

C. R. Barnes

UNITED STATES

POSTAL CARD.

ONE CENT

FORWARDED

NOTHING BUT THE ADDRESS TO BE ON THIS SIDE.

Aug 1887

Walter Deane

Cambridge

York Harbor Maine

Mass

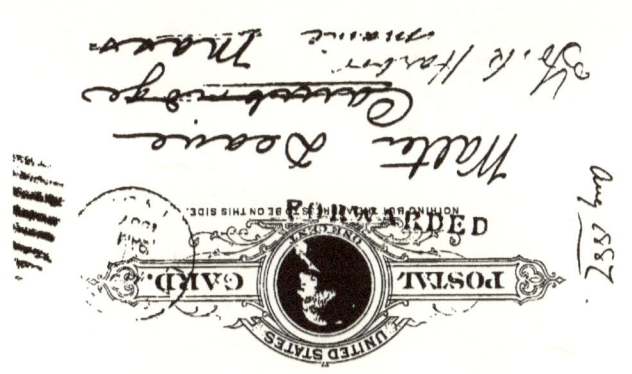

The
Botanical Gazette.
EDITORS:
JOHN M. COULTER,
WABASH COLLEGE, CRAWFORDSVILLE, IND.
CHARLES R. BARNES,
UNIVERSITY OF WISCONSIN, MADISON, WIS.
J. C. ARTHUR,
PURDUE UNIVERSITY, LAFAYETTE, IND.

18 W. Gilman st.,
Oct. 11th 1887.

My dear Deane:—

Have you deserted me? Or have I deserted you? It is quite an "age" since I heard from you.

I think I wrote you just before I left Lafayette, did I not? I left there Sept. 1, staying until the last minute I could spare. Hardly had I got settled here until the news came of the arrival of a fine boy! How I kicked myself for not staying two days longer! But the exact time of such events "no feller can find out" and I had no reason to think it would occur so soon. Trelease's long expectation was a warning to me. He & his wife left St. Louis early. She came here in May and he closed his work by June 1 and came on. Daily—

hourly almost—they expected Mrs. T. to be confined, but it did not happen until June 29!

I did not get to see my wife and youngster for two weeks. It was impossible to get away until the work was under way here. The boy is a fine one — weighed 8½ pounds at birth and has gained steadily since. Mary had a pretty hard time, and on account of the unusual haemorrhage, she has been slow in regaining strength. She is not yet able to travel, though gaining rapidly now. I expect her and the boy in about 2 weeks.

Mother staid at Lafayette with her and shipped the household goods Oct. 1. I am now putting in all my spare time unpacking. Mother will come in a few days and we will get the house in order before Mary comes.

I wrote you at length about our new building. It is progressing rapidly now and the President says will be ready by Jan. 1. We hardly agree with him, and do not expect to get in before March. Not much will be done in it this year. In the mean time my quarters are very comfortable, tho' not commodious. I have my private room in the herbarium room, a general laboratory and three small rooms for advanced lab. and supply room. Besides there is the general lecture room on the first floor.

My work is heavier this term than any other. I have two lectures per week to the biology class, who are using our Plant Dissection for their botanical training; 3 lectures per week to the Pharmacy students on general morphology & physiology of flowering plants. Besides this I have to oversee laboratory work 3 hours per week in the A.M. and 4 hours per week in the P.M. The rest of the laboratory oversight is done by the assistant, Mr. Russell, who also provides material for work. My spare time is however well arranged, so that I have all of Tuesday

A.M. and all of Monday, Wednesday & Friday P.M. After I get settled at home I hope to be able to do some work.

There has recently been allowed to the department of botany $3000 for additional equipment. We already have about 25 microscopes. This appropriation will allow me to supply the dep't abundantly with microscopes and will provide a number of other pieces of apparatus which we need. In a year I expect to be in good shape for work.

Wish you could come and see the place. We have the most beautiful campus I have ever seen and the fame of the town for beautiful situation, scenery and tasteful homes has doubtless reached even to Cambridge in connection with the late Presidential visit.

Give my kindest regards to Mrs. Deane, and believe me

Ever sincerely yours,

C. R. Barnes

The
Botanical Gazette.
EDITORS:
JOHN M. COULTER, WABASH COLLEGE, CRAWFORDSVILLE, IND.
CHARLES R. BARNES, UNIVERSITY OF WISCONSIN, MADISON, WIS.
J. C. ARTHUR, PURDUE UNIVERSITY, LAFAYETTE, IND.

Dec. 10. 1887.

My dear Deane:-

Sad, sad news, indeed, your letter brings- I am looking every day for worse and hardly daring to hope for better news- I have your p.c. also about poor Suksdorf- Do keep me posted about all the Cambridge people. A postal as often as you can get time to write it will be very gratifying- I have only just a moment

to drop you this line—
I will write you a letter soon—

It is useless to send any message to Mrs. Gray, for she must know if she has time to think in these terrible days how deeply the botanists everywhere sympathize with her and how keenly those who knew the good Doctor feel the blow.

Do you remember my telling you when I was in Cambridge about my dreaming that Dr. Gray was paralyzed?

Is this a case for the Society for Psychic Research? —

Mary and Mother wish me to send their kindest regards to you and Mrs. Deane, in which I join.

Ever yours
E. R. Brown

The
Botanical Gazette.

EDITORS:
JOHN M. COULTER,
WABASH COLLEGE, CRAWFORDSVILLE, IND.
CHARLES R. BARNES,
UNIVERSITY OF WISCONSIN, MADISON, WIS.
J. C. ARTHUR,
PURDUE UNIVERSITY, LAFAYETTE, IND.

Dec. 24. 1887.

My dear Deane:- I have been greatly pleased to hear so frequently from you about Cambridge matters. It has been quite a tax upon your time (and pocket-book!) but it has been very satisfactory to know from headquarters just how Dr. Gray was from day to day. The news is all very sad. I cannot say how sorry I am that he is cut off from us before the Flora is completed. It would be bad enough then to lose him but one would feel then that his chef d'ouvre was done.

The photographs you sent came today. They are certainly very good indeed and quite pretty enough to mount and frame, if one only had an herbarium room. Do you know anything about Davenport's photos of Ophioglossaceae? I saw a notice of them in the *Gazette* but the photos were sent to Coulter.

Speaking of photos, did you ever get the "pitray" of your humble servant which was sent to you at Nantucket?

College work closed here on Wednesday last and all this week I have been busy reading papers, examining drawings and working on the Index and January No. of the Gazette. Within the past 48 hours I have written over 50 pp. of MS. on letter size paper! besides a good deal of miscellaneous scribbling — such as this, E.g.! Next week I am going to pitch in hard on Mosses. I have Sandberg's collections from Idaho, up by Pend d'Oreille Lake, Knowlton's from the Yellowstone Park, a collection from Labrador (small), one from Iowa and divers and sundry half-dozens of species from here, there and everywhere to determine! Do you think a week will suffice? Several European correspondents are asking me to exchange, and to save my neck, I cannot get time to catch up with my work. Next term I am going to have much less to do, however. I shall have six lectures per week, three to Pharmics and 3 to Short Course Agriculture men — and I propose to arrange them so as to leave me the afternoon entirely free. Maybe I can get something done then.

The work for the past term has been very pleasant and I am very well pleased with the place and the prospect. Did I write you that an appropriation of $3000 had been made for the further equipment of the bot'l department? — We are not going to get into our new building until about the middle of next term — say Feb. 1. The work has been pushed to the utmost but there was too much to do to allow us to go in this week. Have you heard of L.H. Bailey's windfall? Cornell has been trying to get him away from Michigan but couldn't make the riffle; so in lieu of having him all the time they have employed him to give a 6-weeks course of lectures @ $500! How's that? Bailey will be in the Lecture Bureau yet and getting $200 a night!!

Wisconsin Academy of Sciences meets here next week. Suppose I'll have to attend. This place has the most enormous number of societies, clubs, etc, etc. that make a drain on one's time. Monday night our Shakespere Club meets & we read Cymbeline. Does your Shakespere Club continue?

All pretty well at home. Baby is first rate. My wife has worn herself out on Xmas work and too much social dissipation but is getting better. She will go home for a visit after New Year's. Both she and mother would send regards I know were I writing at home. My kindest regards, with a "Merry Christmas" and heartiest wishes for a "Happy New Year" to you and Mrs Deane.

Ever yours, C.R. Barnes.

The
Botanical Gazette.
EDITORS:
JOHN M. COULTER,
WABASH COLLEGE, CRAWFORDSVILLE, IND.
CHARLES R. BARNES,
UNIVERSITY OF WISCONSIN, MADISON, WIS.
J. C. ARTHUR,
PURDUE UNIVERSITY, LAFAYETTE, IND.

Jan. 20. 1888

My dear Deane:-

I enclose some sketches of a moss which I would be greatly obliged to have compared with plates 331 (Bryum cernuum), 334 (B. inclinatum), 340 (B. Warneum) and 332 (B. lacustre) of the Bryologia Europaea. Let me know which they are most like and how they depart from the corresponding figures in the Bryologia.

The special points to be noticed are habit (1) shape of leaves (2) shape of capsule and relative size of lid (3) character of margin and apex of leaves (4, 5) and the character of inner peristome (6) -

I am over head and ears today with work - Will write you in a few days -

No great hurry about this comparison - Take your time -

I think I've got a new species -

Faithfully yours,

C. R. Barnes

Please return sketches -

My dear Deane:—

I imagine I have been for the past month in very much the same condition as you have found yourself — namely, <u>very busy</u>. Not so busy however but that I have been greatly gratified by the almost daily bulletins that you found time to write about Doctor Gray. You were very good to keep me posted as to the events at Cambridge. It must have been quite a tax on your time to write to so many. But now it is all over! Dear old man! How glad I should have been to see him once more. I have a very late letter from him — its exact date I do not remember now — and I wrote to him inquiring about some books after he was taken sick. Mrs. Gray answered the letter saying simply that Dr. Gray was ill and could not write. From the unsatisfactory nature of the reply I inferred that Dr. Gray had not dictated the letter, but I little dreamed that his illness was so serious.

I am glad that you understood the sketch for the Torrey people. "A regular botanist" indeed! Who more "regular" or enthusiastic than you I would like to know? I shall expect something good when the March Bulletin comes. The editor of the "Western Naturalist" — a semi-amateur, semi-scientific paper issued here — asked me to write a notice of the Dr's life for him. I complied and will send you a copy as soon as issued. Speaking of these things, was not the Editorial in the February Gazette a neat and graceful tribute? It struck me as particularly happy, in both sentiment and expression. That was Coulter's work ~~I am~~ quite sure. At any rate it was not mine. I couldn't do it. Dr. Farlow has a splendid notice of Dr Gray in our March no. Keep an eye out for it.

As to the photo I sent you. I am sorry that it missed you and as soon as I have some others struck off I will send you another.

Part of my "busy-ness" for the past month or more has been due to the working up of the collections of mosses which I brought out with me. Among the Labrador collection I found the Bryum, drawings of which I sent you for comparison. Do not hurry about them. Take your own time. You are not inconveniencing me in the least by the delay; which seems to prey upon you however. For the last two weeks I have been giving all my spare time to making out an order for chemicals, glassware etc. (laboring (?) to spend my $300 appropriation) and to trying the imbedding process described by the Dutch botanist Moll in the January Gazette – My trial has been a perfect success too – I happened to have some onions growing in hyacinth glass so took the root-tips and imbedded them in soft paraffine – With the microtome I was then able to cut a ribbon of sections through the root – Cutting it lengthwise I sliced a root-tip say 1mm. in thickness into 75 sections, arranged in 1, 2, 3 order – Do you know about this "ribbon method"? I've long envied the zoologists, who have used it for several years. Any soft paraffine, melting say at 50°C., will cohere under proper conditions – E.g. if I trim a block of such paraffine into a rectangular block and cut thin slices from its surface with a razor edge parallel to the sides of the block these sections will cohere by their edges to form a ribbon thus:

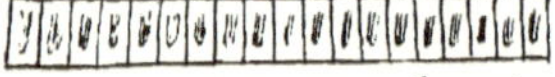

– The imbedding process causes the paraffine to penetrate every part of the tissue and it cuts just like the block itself. Of course the sections are serial and by virtue of the Microtome uniform in thickness. I am going to send you one of my slides soon to show you what can be done in this way. This is especially useful for providing large numbers of sections for class use.

I am quite lonesome at college these days. Dr. Birge who shared the second floor of South Hall with me has moved into his new quarters at Science Hall. I am not going to move until the end of the term (March 28) All the other men have gone into Science Hall and the whole building is occupied now except my rooms.

Did I tell you of our Shakespeare readings this winter? We have had a dozen very pleasant meetings and are to have our last one next Saturday night. The last because the lady at whose house we have been meeting is going to flee from our Wisconsin March, which has an ill reputation. We have read Tempest, Twelfth Night, King John, Henry IV, Cymbeline, Merchant of Venice, Richard III and are to read Henry V on Wednesday. I have enjoyed it very much, and shall be sorry to have the meetings discontinued.

Mary has been at home almost six weeks this winter. She went shortly after the first of January and came back last week. Her mother is very low with consumption and is hardly expected to live longer than a few weeks. Of course it was very hard for Mary to come back but the Doctor and all thought she would better come away for a week. She herself has not been at all strong since the baby was born. Poor girl, she has had enough in the past year and a half to break a stronger constitution than hers. Last December (a year ago) you know her father was taken seriously ill (a stroke of paralysis we now believe it) from which he has never wholly recovered; then her mother returned from the Bermudas in March sick and has gradually run into the disease which is killing her; then in April our dear little boy died and it has been a constant struggle with her to control herself about that and her mother's illness; then she suffered such a terrible physical drain when the baby was born — a hemorrhage that nearly sapped her life — that it is small wonder she is not well! She is about all the time and able to take a great deal of the care of the baby but cannot do much walking and suffers so with pain in her eyes that she cannot read. We take a

short stroll almost every day
when the weather is pleasant.
We have board walks here
which free themselves quickly
of snow and ice, so that getting
about is quite comfortable.
The baby is as fat and hearty
and good as a baby can be.
I think he grows more and more
like Eddie. By the way, Eddie was
just two or three months over
three years old when the picture you have was taken. It
was taken about Dec. 1. 1886. He
was born Sept. 10. 1883.

Mary sends her warmest
regards to you both to which
I add mine. If mother were down
I am sure she too would join with
us. Let me hear from you as
often as you find time. By
the way, if you can get them
conveniently wont you send me
the newspaper abstracts of Goodale's forestry lectures?

Ever sincerely yours,

C. R. Barnes

Mch 8 – '88

Dear Deane:– As a reward of merit I send you photo today, with hearty thanks for the study of Bryum drawings – Will write you soon –

Ever B.

NOTHING BUT THE ADDRESS TO BE ON THIS SIDE.

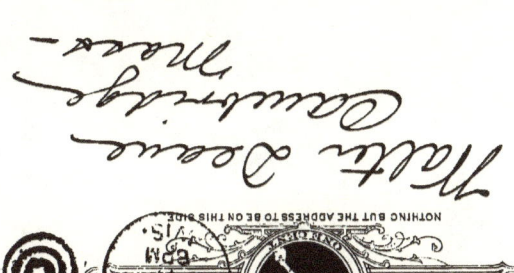

Walter Deane
Cambridge
Mass.

Mch. 15/1888.

My dear Deane:—I send you by this mail a copy of the Annual—You may not get the full force of its fun but will appreciate the information about the Univ.

Ever yrs C.R.B—

NOTHING BUT THE ADDRESS TO BE ON THIS SIDE.

Mr. Walter Deane
Cambridge
Mass.

The
Botanical Gazette.

EDITORS:

JOHN M. COULTER,
WABASH COLLEGE, CRAWFORDSVILLE, IND.

CHARLES R. BARNES,
UNIVERSITY OF WISCONSIN, MADISON, WIS.

J. C. ARTHUR,
PURDUE UNIVERSITY, LAFAYETTE, IND.

Trelease writes me he is planning to sail for Europe on June 2.

March 28. 1888.

My dear Deane:-

We are just thro' the final faculty-meeting of this term and I embrace the first hour of vacation to write to you. I ought to have written at once on hearing of your desire to come to see some of your Western friends at the Easter recess, and urged you to do so. But I am sure that you would not hesitate to come without urging, for you know how very glad I would be to see you. I would rather though that you would come in the summer and let me show you all the beauties of Madison — when you could stay long enough to make it worth while coming so far.

Can you and Mrs. Deane not take your summering in the great Northwest this year, instead of at Rye Beach and Nantucket? I do wish you would plan to come out this way and give us a share of your time.

The picture of Dr. Gray came a few days ago, when I was in the midst of moving — not my household gods but my scientific ones — so that I did not write at once to thank you for it. You must know how glad I am to get it. I think it very good indeed, though the expression strikes me as a trifle sadder than was his wont. I suppose it is the one the Torrey people are to reproduce.

Did you see the photogravure of the Bronze ~~tablet~~ Medallion of Dr. G. in the "Garden and Forest"? It is superb and I intend framing it. It will pay you to send for the Vol. I. No. 2 if you would care at all for it. By the way, the G. & F. promises to be a most admirable journal and has a great deal of botanical matter in it.

As I indicated a few lines back I have moved my quarters from the old South Hall to the new Science Hall. A most agreeable change it is too, especially because of the greater elbow-room, more modern conveniences and the new floors of hard pine. The South Hall was the first of the University buildings and was long used as a Dormitory. The floors were of soft pine so dry and friable that a pile of dust would accumulate under ones table from the simple shuffling of feet for one day. No matter how much it was swept a second sweeping would yield ...

of the floor as the first! Of course the mere passing around the room kept everything dusty and it was fearfully hard on lenses.

The moving was a good deal of a job. The herbarium (some 8000 species + duplicates) had to be bundled up and put into boxes where it is to stay until the cases are rejuvenated. Then there was a "sight" of stuff which accumulates around a laboratory. The men were two days, Saturday & Monday, in getting the things down. I shall be some weeks in having them put into place, I fear. However enough is arranged to allow students to begin work again on the 5th prox. and to allow me to spend my vacation on mosses. I took care to keep _them_ separate from the general herbarium. I am going to take up today a package of Anderson's from

Montana, which has been on hands since Sept. last.

Speaking of Mosses reminds me that I had word the other day from Cardot to whom I sent a specimen of that Bryum you looked up for me, saying that he thought it a new species too. He sent it to Philibert who has made a specialty of Bryum and said he would communicate P's opinion.

I have been forgetting to ask Mr. Russell about making the slides for you. Maybe he would undertake it. I send you by this mail one of my root-tip slides. You can study in it very nicely the division of the nucleus. The ~~left~~ rt hand one is the second section from ~~to the side~~ ~~of~~ the center of the root-tip. Altho these are 1/2000 of an inch they are a little too thick for the best dis-

play of the general structure.
I have some onion leaves "in transitu" now and will send you some sections of stomata if I get good ones.

I send you too by this mail a picture of our baby. The smile is quite normal and characteristic of him –

I meant to have written you earlier too about the sketch in Torr. Bull. I enjoyed it very much indeed – every one gets at some new points. Yours was especially interesting in regard to his European trips. The whole "does you proud". I hope if you have separate copies you will send me one with the portrait. I want to get all the sketches of the Dr. together.

The Apr. Gazette will contain a posthumous paper on some new or rare species — his last botanical "contribution" –

Many thanks for the synopses of Goodale's lectures. They must be tiptop. Regards always to Mrs. Deane.

The
Botanical Gazette.
EDITORS:
JOHN M. COULTER,
WABASH COLLEGE, CRAWFORDSVILLE, IND.
CHARLES R. BARNES,
UNIVERSITY OF WISCONSIN, MADISON, WIS.
J. C. ARTHUR,
PURDUE UNIVERSITY, LAFAYETTE, IND.

April 14. 1888.

My dear Deane:—

May I send you another photo of myself without magnifying myself? One of the photographers here asked for a sitting to make some pictures for the Pharmacy class (which leaves at the end of the 2nd term) and the result is so much the best likeness I have ever had taken — so my family say — that I beg leave to send you one. I hope you will destroy the other one I sent you this winter and replace it by

to be very useful to me some day.

As you have been working for Bebb you will be interested to know (in case you do not already know) that he is getting ready a number of articles for the *Gazette*. I have in hand a double plate for him. Have you seen any of his drawings? He is a most exquisite draughtsman. I wish I could draw *half* as well! Every line is as steady and true as an engraving. He aspired — so he puts it — "to draw with a pen but after trying it writes: "My ambition to become a pen-and-ink delineator of plants has collapsed — gone up — faded into thin air!" He could not stand the nervous strain of driving a sharp pointed pen over paper.

You will be interested to hear that our Board of Regents at their April meeting adopted a scheme for 8 *fellowships* — four to be filled this year and four next. Each is of $400, quite sufficient to "keep" a man here in comfort. One hour's instruction per day will be required of each fellow: the remainder of his time he is to devote to study in his special department. The grant of a fellowship may be renewed once if approved by the Faculty. We shall thus I hope be able to hold our best men here for a year or two after graduation and perhaps attract others from other institutions. The U. of W. is thus the first institution west of the Alleghanies (unless you count Cornell *west*) to adopt the fellowship system. That and the beginning of the "Seminar" plan I consider two good steps for one year.

I have a good letter from Kennedy telling me about the sad year he has had. How he does fly back and forth across the Atlantic!

Mosses continue to pile in upon me. I have just received a package of 70 spp. from Leiberg up at Lake Pend d'Oreille in Idaho. From what he writes I judge that he is in a most prolific region for mosses. He has already collected about 110 spp. in his neighborhood.

I may say to you, inter nos, that I have definitely determined to undertake a Manual of the mosses. There has already come in a good amount of new material since L. & J.'s work & something is needed badly to facilitate study of mosses. L. & J. only muddle & discourage beginners or amateurs.

Warm spring day. I write by an open window and am too warm. Ice gone out of 3d lake; still floating in 4th. Regards to Mrs. Deane.

Ever sincerely yours, C.R.B.

The
Botanical Gazette.
EDITORS:
JOHN M. COULTER,
WABASH COLLEGE, CRAWFORDSVILLE, IND.
CHARLES R. BARNES,
UNIVERSITY OF WISCONSIN, MADISON, WIS.
J. C. ARTHUR,
PURDUE UNIVERSITY, LAFAYETTE, IND.

April 26. 1888.

My dear Deane: I can only drop you a line this A.M. about binding Gazette

From motives of economy I had Vol. XI & XII bound together, keeping front cover only on. Between the volumes is a stiff green or blue sheet. Index is placed at end of each volume, table of Contents at front. With this arrangement my volume is less than 2 in thick, and not unwieldy.

My 10-vol. index I had bound in blue cloth & it slips in at end of 10th vol. where its blue back makes it conspicuous enough to be easily found.

What does Goodale's appointment mean? That he is to live at the Garden & that there will be no systematist at the head of the Herb.? Always excepting Watson who of course will be Curator– I hope they will get some one to do the manual labor and let W. have time to work.

M. W. Bailey *is* a *curious chap*! He is one to whom the miner's phrase "*Down on his luck*" strictly applies– *Blue*? Shades of Indigo!!

Hurrah for L. H. B——!

In haste but ever

Yours, C. R. Barnes

The
Botanical Gazette.

EDITORS:
JOHN M. COULTER,
WABASH COLLEGE, CRAWFORDSVILLE, IND.
CHARLES R. BARNES,
UNIVERSITY OF WISCONSIN, MADISON, WIS.
J. C. ARTHUR,
PURDUE UNIVERSITY, LAFAYETTE, IND.

May 18. 1888.

My dear Deane:—

I was very glad to get the copy of your paper on Dr. Gray a few days ago and today the picture. I have ordered an extra one to frame for the herbarium room here, for I think it most excellent. I believe I like it better even than the photo taken in March. Do you know when this was taken? You were very kind to send me a copy of the article. I did not know that you had it reprinted. Supposed of course the Bulletin furnished you extra copies as we do. I fear your extravagance in printing this laid quite in the shade your extravagance in buying the Engelmann volume, and even my latest extravagance ~~of~~ the purchase of a fly rod for fishing!

I am grinding away at an address for the Alumni Ass. at Hanover on June 12, which I was flattered into assenting to give. I spend two or three weeks of my valuable(?) time, cudgeling my brains to get up a speech on some subject that I know nothing about — so as to have it suitable for the occasion, forsooth! — and then pay $30 (in expenses) for the privilege of delivering it! "Ah! fool, fool! great is thy folly!" But I would not mind the "grinding" if it were not grinding with an empty hopper — so empty that the stones cut themselves —

Hasn't Bailey fallen on his feet though? $3000 + Europe! Whew!

Now to keep myself from envy I'll recount my mercies to you! I have just ordered complete sets of the Bot. Zeitung, Pringsheim's Jahrbücher, Cohn's Beiträge, Arbeiten der bot. Inst. Würzburg, Untersuchungen aus dem bot. Inst. Tübingen, Ray Society Memoirs, the Bryologia Europaea, Hedwig's works, Schwägrichen's Species Muscorum, the Annales des Sciences Naturelles (Botanique) from Sér. IV. and a lot of individual books to the amount of about $750.

Did I tell you too that I have ordered a lot of physiological apparatus ~~too~~? Ah, well, it is a pleasure to spend others money if you can't have it yourself. With what apparatus and library we have we shall be pretty well fixed for good work. You can depend upon it that I laid in a good stock of Moss books!

Mary told me long ago to explain to Mrs. Deane why she did not write and I have kept forgetting it. Her eyes have been paining her so whenever she tries to use them that she has had to desist entirely from reading sewing or writing. I ~~even~~ have to write even her letters to her father and sister at her dictation. Tell Mrs. D. that Mary appreciated her letter highly and would long ago have answered it but for this. She improves slowly, but we have as yet had no weather fit to go out in. It is cold and very rainy & has been all this month.

Circular of Information.

University of Wisconsin.

NEW SCIENCE HALL.

MADISON, WISCONSIN.

1888.

University of Wisconsin.

SPECIAL COURSES FOR NORMAL GRADUATES.

To afford graduates of the State Normal Schools facilities for extending their studies advantageously, and, at the same time, to attain a recognized standing leading to a degree, without loss of time or inconvenience arising from the want of adjustment of their previous studies to the standard college courses, the following special courses have been adopted by the University. To these courses the regular graduates from the advanced courses of the State Normal Schools of Wisconsin will be admitted with the rank of Juniors. Two years of successful study will enable the graduates to complete one of the courses, and, by a proper selection of studies, to graduate with the degree of Bachelor of Letters (English Course) or of Bachelor of Science.

The courses presented are essentially elective, but if regular graduation and a degree are sought, the range of election is restricted in important particulars. It is felt that in all but exceptional cases the greatest benefit will be secured by protracted study in definite lines, since the previous courses of the candidates have consisted of a somewhat wide range of relatively short studies. The student rarely becomes possessed of the real life and spirit of a language, a science or a philosophy, except through prolonged, continuous study. The acquisition of this deeper vital insight is deemed of supreme importance to the truest scholarship. The requirements imposed, however, but partially enforce this view; they are rather the minimum of consecutive specialized work that can be accepted of candidates for the respective degrees. Purely elective courses may be taken by those who do not seek degrees.

For the degree of Bachelor of Letters (English Course) continuous studies running through at least one year will be required in civics, in ancient or modern language, and in science. Similar courses in history, literature and philosophy are recommended. Those who have not previously taken the Latin offered in the Normal Schools, will be required to take a two-years' course in some foreign language, preferably German or French. Latin cannot be taken, as the University offers no elementary classes in that language. Those who have previously taken Latin, will be expected to take at least an additional years' course in language, preferably Latin, German or French. A continuous two-years' course is recommended. Greek may be taken. Three full studies will be required throughout the course, those additional to the above being elective. These may be selected from any of the studies offered by the University which the students' preparation and the schedule of recitations permit. Extra studies may be taken by those whose standing and strength justify it.

To attain the degree of Bachelor of Science, three courses of one year each in selected sciences, and two courses of one year each in ancient or modern language are required. A course of two years is regarded not only as the equivalent of two courses of one year each, but as generally preferable to the latter, especially in language. Those who have taken no previous classical or foreign language, will be required to take two courses of two years each in foreign language. In this case Latin cannot be taken for want of an elementary course. German and French are recommended. In addition to the above requirements, elective studies sufficient to constitute three full studies throughout the course are required.

The regular rhetorical work of the college classes will be required of students in these courses.

Normal graduates who may have a sufficient knowledge of Latin, French or German, in addition to the full acquirements of Normal school graduates, may become candidates for the degree of Bachelor of Letters (Modern Classical Course), in which case they will be permitted to take such subcourses as will be the nearest available equivalents of those of the Modern Classical Course.

COURSES FOR NORMAL GRADUATES LEADING TO THE DEGREE OF BACHELOR OF LETTERS (ENGLISH COURSE).

JUNIOR YEAR.

I. LANGUAGE (Latin, French or German) pursued continuously throughout the year.

II. CIVICS, (Elementary Law, English and American Constitutional Law, Political Economy) pursued continuously throughout the year.

III. SCIENCE, (Chemistry, Physics, Mathematics, Astronomy, Botany, Mineralogy, or Geology) pursued continuously throughout the year.

IV. ELECTIVES, one or more of the above long courses may be deferred until the Senior year, and elective studies substituted therefor.

V. RHETORICAL WORK, five essays or theses and one oration during the year.

SENIOR YEAR.

I. LANGUAGE, (Latin, French or German) pursued continuously throughout the year.

II. HISTORY, a course embracing one or more of the following is recommended: History of Modern Institutions, History of Civilization, Dynastic and Territorial History, English Constitutional History, Archæology, advanced American or English History.

III. ENGLISH, elective, a course in English Masterpieces and Early English is recommended to those who chose Latin instead of English Literature in the Normal School course.

IV. CIVICS, the required long course in civics may be taken during this year. Additional elective studies in civics may also be taken.

V. SCIENCE, the required long course in science may be taken during this year. Additional elective studies in science may also be taken.

VI. RHETORICAL WORK, three essays or theses, and one oration are required during the fall and winter terms.

COURSES FOR NORMAL GRADUATES LEADING TO THE DEGREE OF BACHELOR OF SCIENCE.

JUNIOR YEAR.

I. SCIENCE. (1). A continuous course in Chemistry, Physics, Mathematics or Astronomy throughout the year.

(2). A continuous course in Botany, Zoology or Mineralogy throughout the year.

(3). Mineralogy may be taken during the second half of winter term and through the spring term preparatory to Geology in the Senior year. One of these courses in science may be taken in the Senior year, but if Zoology is elected, courses in Chemistry, Mineralogy or Physics, or in Zoology or Botany should be taken during the Junior year.

II. LANGUAGE, (Latin, German or French) pursued throughout the year. Students who chose English Literature in the Normal course will be required to take two courses in language throughout the year.

III. ELECTIVES. If either course in science is deferred until the Senior year, elective studies are to be substituted. Extra elective studies may also be taken by those prepared for them.

IV. RHETORICAL WORK, five essays or theses, and one oration during the year.

SENIOR YEAR.

I. SCIENCE, a continuous study running through the year. If Geology is chosen as one of the three required courses, it should be taken during this year, and be preceded by the two other courses in science.

II. LANGUAGE, (Latin, German or French) throughout the year. Students who chose English Literature in the Normal course will be required to take two courses in language throughout the year.

III. ELECTIVE STUDIES, sufficient to make at least three full studies.

IV. RHETORICAL WORK, three essays or theses, and one oration during the fall and winter terms.

UNIVERSITY BUILDINGS.

Circular of Information.

University of Wisconsin.

NEW SCIENCE HALL.

MADISON, WISCONSIN.

1888.

University of Wisconsin.

THE University of Wisconsin offers thirteen formal courses of study, embracing the Ancient Classical, Modern Classical, General Science, and English Courses; a Special Civic-historical Course antecedent to the study of Law and Journalism; a Special Science Course antecedent to the study of Medicine, and professional and technical courses in Law, Agriculture, Civil, Mechanical, Mining and Metallurgical Engineering and Pharmacy. In connection with these courses many elective studies are offered, by selecting from which students may, in considerable measure, shape for themselves courses, especially in the Junior and Senior years. The number of possible courses thus offered is very large. Special students are allowed much liberty in the choice of studies.

Exrellent facilities for post-graduate study and investigation are offered.

There are three methods of admission to the University: **First, by examination at the University; second, by special local examination under the supervision of an authorized agent of the University; and third, by presentation of a proper certificate from an accredited school.**

I. **The Regular Examinations** at the University are two in number, one in June (14th and 15th), and the other in September (4th and 5th). The earlier examination is intended for those who wish to set at rest all doubt respecting admission, while fresh upon their studies, and for those who wish to test their qualifications at an early date that they may have time to make up deficiencies, if necessary. The September examination immediately precedes the opening of the fall term.

II. To save expense and embarrassment to those who live at a distance, **Special Local Examinations** will be given when satisfactory arrangements can be made. Upon request, questions will be sent to any Principal or County Superintendent who will consent to supervise the examination for the accommodation of the candidate, and return the answers to the University. It will be left with the candidate to make the necessary arrangements with the Principal or Superintendent.

III. Graduates of **Accredited Schools** will be received on the recommendation of the Principal without examination; also students of accredited schools who may be especially recommended by the Principal.

REQUIREMENTS FOR ADMISSION.

1. General Examination for all Candidates for the Freshman Class: Orthography, grammar, sentential analysis, arithmetic, algebra through quadratics, plane geometry, civil and physical geography, U. S. history.

2. For the Ancient Classical Course, the above, and ancient and English history; Latin grammar and composition, Caesar (four books), Cicero (six orations), Virgil (six books), Sallust's Conspiracy of Catilline; Greek grammar and composition, Xenophon's Anabasis (three books), Homer's Iliad (two books).

3. For the Modern Classical Course, all the above (1) and (2), except Greek, instead of which German grammar and twenty lessons in any standard German reader, and solid geometry are required.

4. For the English Course, the general examination required of all (1), and English literature, ancient and English history, botany, physiology, natural philosophy and solid geometry.

5. For the General Science, Special Science (pre-medical), Long Agricultural, and all Engineering Courses, the general examination required of all (1), and German grammar, twenty lessons in German reader, botany, physiology, natural philosophy and solid geometry.

6. For the Civic-Historic Course, the same as for the English or Classical Courses.

7. For the Elementary Greek Class (Greek not required), Latin grammar and composition, Caesar (four books), Cicero (two orations), Sallust's Conspiracy of Catilline, ancient and English history, and the general examination required of all (1).

8. For Special Students, the English branches required for the General Science Course including the general examination (1).

9. For Law and Pharmacy, evidence of sufficient education to profitably pursue the courses.

The Faculty embraces upwards of fifty instructors. The laboratories are new, extensive and well equipped, embracing the chemical, physical, metallurgical, mineralogical, geological, zoological, botanical, civil and mechanical engineering, agricultural and pharmaceutical laboratories. Seminaries for advanced study in history, language, literature, mathematics, and other branches are being developed.

The libraries accessible to students embrace that of the University, 16,000 volumes; of the State Historical Society, 123,000 volumes; of the State Law Department, 20,000 volumes; of the City, 9,000 volumes, besides special professional and technical libraries, thus affording very exceptional opportunities for reading and special research. The Washburn Observatory; the Students Observatory; the Agricultural Experiment Station, and the bacteriological and other special laboratories afford unusual facilities for original investigation. The general appointments of the University are of a high order.

The fall term opens September the 5th. Catalogues sent on application to the Secretary or President.

UNIVERSITY BUILDINGS.

University of Wisconsin.

SPECIAL SCIENCE COURSE, ANTECEDENT TO THE STUDY OF MEDICINE.

In response to a request from the Wisconsin State Medical Society, the University offers the following Special Course in Science, arranged for those contemplating the study of medicine and surgery. It is intended to give a broad and solid foundation for the professional medical course, together with collegiate culture.

The Chicago College of Physicians and Surgeons, Rush Medical College, and the Chicago Medical College have approved the course and will accept it as the equivalent of one year's study, thus enabling those who have taken the four years' course here to complete their medical course in these excellent colleges in two years.

All the studies given cannot be taken in the time allotted. Three full studies are required during each term, which may be chosen from those given. If the degree of Bachelor of Science is sought the *required* studies of the General Science Course must be taken.

From the branches offered, special students may select a two years' course embracing the larger portion of those subjects which bear directly upon the studies of medicine and surgery. A more liberal course, however, is recommended, which shall embrace not only all of these sciences, but cognate branches and a due measure of language and of mental science, substantially as outlined in the following course.

FRESHMAN YEAR.

FALL TERM.

PHARMACEUTICAL BOTANY, subcourse VIII, *three-fifths study*.
ZOOLOGY, subcourse I, Morphology, *full study*.
BOTANY, subcourse II, Morphology, *full study*.
GERMAN or FRENCH, Elementary or advanced, *full or half study*.
MATHEMATICS, subcourse I, Algebra, *full study*.

WINTER TERM.

PHARMACEUTICAL BOTANY, subcourse VIII, *three-fifths study.*
ZOOLOGY, subcourse I, Morphology, *full study.*
ZOOLOGY, subcourse II, General, *full study.*
MATHEMATICS, subcourse II, Theory of Equations, *full study.*
GERMAN or FRENCH, continued.

SPRING TERM.

BOTANY, subcourse I, Morphology of Flowering Plants. Lectures, Laboratory work and collection, *full study.*
ZOOLOGY, subcourse I, Morphology, *full study.*
ZOOLOGY, subcourse II, General, *full study.*
MATHEMATICS, subcourse IV, Trigonometry, *full study.*
GERMAN or FRENCH, continued.

SOPHOMORE YEAR.

FALL TERM.

VERTEBRATE ANATOMY, subcourse IV (Zoology), *full study.*
CHEMISTRY, subcourse I, Descriptive Inorganic, *full study.*
BOTANY, subcourse II, General Morphology, *full study.*
MECHANICS, subcourse I, *three-fifths study.*
GERMAN or FRENCH.

WINTER TERM.

ZOOLOGY, subcourse IV, Vertebrate Anatomy, *full study.*
CHEMISTRY, subcourse I, Qualitative Analysis, *two-fifths or full study.*
BOTANY, subcourse IV, Vegetable Histology, *ten hours a week.*
BOTANY, subcourse III, General Vegetable Morphology, *ten hours a week.*
PHYSICS, subcourse I, *four-fifths study.*
GERMAN or FRENCH, continued.

SPRING TERM.

ZOOLOGY, subcourse VII, Animal Embryology, *full study.*
CHEMISTRY, subcourse I, Qualitative Analysis, *two-fifths or full study.*
BOTANY, subcourse IV, Vegetable Histology, *ten hours a week.*
BOTANY, subcourse III, General Vegetable Morphology, *full study.*
PHYSICS, subcourse I, *four-fifths study.*
GERMAN or FRENCH, continued.

JUNIOR YEAR.

FALL TERM.

BOTANY, subcourse V, Vegetable Embryology and Physiology, *ten hours a week.*
ZOOLOGY, subcourse VI, Human Physiology, *three-fifths study.*
Subcourse V, Animal Histology, *full study.*
CHEMISTRY, subcourse II, Descriptive Organic Chemistry, *full study half the term.*
CHEMISTRY, subcourse III, Quantitative Analysis, Volumetric and Gravimetric, *full or partial study.*
PHARMACEUTICAL CHEMISTRY, subcourse I, *three-fifths study.*
EXPERIMENTAL PHYSICS, subcourse II, *six hours a week.*

WINTER TERM.

BOTANY, subcourse V, Vegetable Physiology, *ten hours a week.*
ZOOLOGY, subcourse VI, Human Physiology, *three-fifths study.*
BACTERIOLOGY, subcourse I, *full study.*
CHEMISTRY, subcourse III, Quantitative Analysis, *full or partial study.*
PHARMACEUTICAL CHEMISTRY, subcourse II, *three-fifths study.*
EXPERIMENTAL PHYSICS, subcourse II, *six hours a week.*

SPRING TERM.

BOTANY, subcourse V, Vegetable Physiology, *ten hours a week.*
ZOOLOGY, subcourse IX, Advanced Histology or Bacteriology, *full study.*
ORGANIC CHEMISTRY, subcourses II and V, *full or partial study.*
TOXICOLOGY AND URINE ANALYSIS, subcourse V, *part term studies.*

SENIOR YEAR.

FALL TERM.

CHEMISTRY, subcourses III and V, Advanced work, organic and inorganic, *amount optional.*
ZOOLOGY, subcourse IX, Advanced and original work, *full study.*
BOTANY, subcourse VI, Advanced and original work, *full study.*
MINERALOGY, subcourse I, Blowpipe Analysis, *three-fifths study.**
GEOLOGY, subcourses I and II or III, *full or three-fifths study.*
PSYCHOLOGY, subcourse I, *full study.*

WINTER TERM.

CHEMISTRY, subcourses III and V, Advanced work, organic or inorganic, *amount optional.*
ZOOLOGY, subcourse IX, Advanced and original work, *full study.*
BOTANY, subcourse VI, Advanced and original work, *full study.*
GEOLOGY, subcourse II, long course, *full study.*

SPRING TERM.

CHEMISTRY, subcourses III and V, Advanced work, organic and inorganic, *amount optional.*
ZOOLOGY, subcourse IX, Advanced and original work, *full study.*

* Mineralogy should be taken in the Junior Year if the long course in Geology is contemplated.

BOTANY, subcourse VI. Advanced and original work, *full study*.

Rhetorical work and military drill required as of other students.

Students completing the *required studies* of the General Science Course (which see), and sufficient of the foregoing to make a total of thirty-nine terms' work during the course will be entitled to the degree of Bachelor of Science.

Catalogues sent on application to the President or Secretary.

MADISON, WIS., U. S. A. July 5. 1888.

My dear Deane:- I have been meaning to write to you for a long while, but one thing and another has caused a postponement until I was stirred up by your letter of inquiry, which came yesterday - I specially intended writing to urge you to consider a trip to Madison among your summer journeys - Can't you come out here say about Aug. 1 and stay till the meeting of the A^{S}S on the 15th? Then we would take a steamer at Milwaukee and go around the lakes to Cleveland - How does that strike you? Do it. When I say you I use the 2nd person plural to include Mrs. Deane, to whom Mary would send a special message were she here. I as her vice-gerent(!) particularly urge Mrs. Deane to persuade you into this scheme -

The busi-ness which prevented my writing for so long was, as I think I wrote you, the preparation of a speech for the meeting of the Alumni Ass^{n} of my Alma Mater - By dint of grinding I got it done in time and a more unsuitable thing for the purpose was never concocted. On June 8th Mary Mother and the boy left Madison with me. Mother parted from us at Chicago to go to Piqua, O. to visit a brother & sister there. Mary and I went on to Lafayette where I stopped over Sunday. Monday afternoon I went to Indianapolis, to stay overnight with cousins and expected to leave at 8:15 A.M. for Madison (Ind.). But the train had changed time to 8 and I was consequently left! As there was no other train by which I could get to Hanover, my destination, before 9 o'clock at night, my address had to be postponed! I delivered it Wednesday evening however. The night was exceedingly hot & people were tired so that I don't think I covered myself with glory to any extent!

I did not stop at Lafayette coming back. Mary met me at the train and we had a few minutes together. Since then I have not seen her and you can imagine that I am rather lonesome — with all the family gone. As soon as I got back I had to plunge into examinations and then Commencement was upon us. On the 20th I went up to Ripon, Wis. and delivered an address before the Biological Society, using the same one as for the Alumni Assn. For this purpose it was more suitable and as I felt it to be so it was delivered better and seemed to "take" pretty well. On the 28th I went back to Ripon to tell the State Hort.

UNIVERSITY OF WISCONSIN,
Botanical Laboratory.
CHARLES R. BARNES, Professor of Botany
MADISON, WIS., U. S. A.

Soc. 'how roots forage'. I stayed there two days. The between-times have been filled up with work on my mosses, varnishing my boat and fitting up a boathouse, rowing, fishing and loafing. I try to stay away from the house as much as possible. Fishing is poor just now but will pick up again soon. I was out yesterday morning and took a 10-mile pull, down to Merrill Springs and back. The shores of the lake are beautiful in many places. Down that way one can row in the shade of a rocky cliff covered with clinging vines & shrubs. Among the latter Lonicera flava is particularly noticeable by reason of the glaucous upper leaves. They are so white that they look almost like disks of grey paper. While pulling along I had out a line trolling a fly, but neither fly, spoon nor minnow proved attractive enough to induce the fish to rise. One white bass and one perch attacked it and that was not worth speaking of. But pretty soon the pickerel will begin to get hungry — then look out! Come out & try your luck!

My intention is now to stay in Madison for the summer. July 10 to Aug. 10 our Summer school for teachers is in operation and I shall teach in that for an hour or so per day. Mary and mother are to return next week for the summer. A friend from Lafayette will accompany them to stay a week or two. Aside from her we shall have no other visitors till you and Mrs. Deane come. I very much hope that your "Aug. address" will be #10 W. Gilman St., Madison, Wis.

The mosses that you send are pretty "tough." I recognize in the mélange five species of Hypnum, a hepatic and a lichen. The only two species recognizable with certainty are Hypnum reptile and H. Crista. The others I can't even guess at as they are so young that they may be almost anything. The bird evidently saw a nice little flat patch of green and pulled it up bodily. The lichen came with it. Perhaps F. L. Sargent, Boston (c/ B. L. Bray) can name it. The hepatic I will look up at noon in Underwood's Cat. & possibly can name it or at least give the genus. I enclose the named forms so you can see what proportion of the cover is made up of them.

With warmest regards to Mrs. Deane

Faithfully yours, C. R. Barnes

Madison, Wis., August 25. 1888.

My dear Deane:--

You here and now have ocular evidence that I have a writing machine. I was rash enough to expend a part of my earnings in the summmer school in the purchase of a Caligraph. I operated one of these machines for some time a few years ago but I find that much of my former skill has departed. I believe however that I can even now write faster with it than with a pen. Of the accuracy you yourself can judge.

I got your last letter just before I started for the meeting of the AAAS at Cleveland so that I could not look at the specimen you sent for examination. Since getting back I have been as busy as a bee writing up the account of the meeting for the Gazette. I have taken a look at the stuff and can make nothing out of it. Whatever it is it does not belong to my bailiwick. I think that there is a Hepatic that has such a form. Send it to Underwood and ask him about it.

We had a very pleasant meeting of the association, though the attendance was smaller than usual. Only about 400 registered, while the attendance runs from 500 to 600 as a general thing. About 60 registered in the botanical club. It is to be remembered however that these include a number of hangers-on rather than botanists. So far a I can recall there were but TWO botanists from east of the Hudson river. You ought to be ashamed of yourselves! Why under the sun don't you get up enough spunk to come to some of the meetings? If you would once get to a meeting you would make a business of coming to succeeding ones. A man like you who loves to meet the botanists he has corresponded with or knows by reputation can not fail to derive solid satisfaction from the meetings. Of course it is the social feature which is prominent and properly so, I think. You could doubtless get more information by sitting down at home and reading some of the standard books. I am very sure that the information which you would have gotten from the last meeting would be exceeded in accuracy by the poorest of the text-books. ------ I am not going to write you an account of the meeting for I have just finished doing that for the September GAZETTE and I cannot afford to do it twice so close together even for your sake.

Just before I went to the association I had a 3-days fishnic. Owen, our professor of French, has a schooner-rigged sail-boat with accommodations for four. We, i.e., Owen, Parker, our professor of music, Bunn, judge of the U.S. court, and I went off to the best fishing grounds and anchored there. We slept on the boat and spent the most of the day in fishing. We would get up at about four o'clock and fish till breakfast-time; then eat our breakfast and fish till ten or 11 o'clock; then come in and play whist or 'gas' till dinner. Owen had a camp kit along and we cooked some of our fish for dinner. About three o'clock we would start out again and fish till 7 or 8. It goes without saying that we had a jolly good time. The fishing was not good except on one day. Our total catch amounted to about 125lbs. Most of them were pickerel -- not your eastern pond pickerel but a fish whose flesh is exceedingly sweet and delicate. The largest of the catch weighed 10.5lbs. My largest weighed only 6 but he was a fighter and it took 15 minutes to land him,in the course of which he made 3 magnificent jumps clear of the water. The largest of the other fish was a 5lb. black bass. We also caught numbers of white bass,but they don't count in fishing annals here though they are fine for eating. They rarely weigh more than a pound,but for their weight are quite gamey.

Aside from these episodes my life this summer has been entirely uneventful. The work of the summer school proved as pleasant as any such work ever is,and it sufficed to supply me with several luxuries which I should not have been justified in buying else.

The family continue in about their usual health.The baby is as well as he can be and a very good child. He is the pet of the neighborhood just as Eddie was. Mary continues to improve though slowly. She is still troubled with her eyes and the oculist who examined her assured her that it was wholly due to her anaemic condition and that she would get her strength back everywhere else before her e eyes came back to their normal condition. The optic nerve,he said, was as white as a sheet of paper.

We expect to move again! Prof.Owen has just built a new house near the University and we improve our condition by the move, especially as regards storage room and yard room. We shall also be nearer to the University and on the lake shore.

Write me of your doings this summer. Now you can just begin to make your plans to come out here next summer for I am going to have you nolens volens! This is just as good a summer resort as there is on the Maine coast and the cost of railroad fare will be offset by your free entertainment! With regards to Mrs.D.from us all,

Ever yours, Charles R. Barnes

Madison, Wis., December 7.1888.

My dear Deane:--

Well, well; what lax correspondents we are getting to be. You let my letter go unanswered for two months and now I have done as badly by you. Who would have believed it ?

Busy ? I've been so busy lately that I could hardly tell whether I was on my head or my heels, without stopping to think about it. With my usual procrastinating policy I put off making the index of the Gazette by numbers, as it came, so that I have had the whole of the year to do at once.

Then I have offered a course in experimental vegetable physiology this year, and, as I have no handbook at command in this subject, I have been compelled to prepare a schedule of experiments myself. Fortunately I have a copy of Detmer's Pflanzen-physiologisches Praktikum lately issued, and by translating the experiments in that (such as were suitable) and by picking out additional ones from Sachs' Experimental-Pflanzenphysiologie, Goodale's Praxis and Vines' Lectures, I have succeeded in keeping the class busy so far. Fortunately too, the class is small and its personnel such that I can practice on it without detriment. Several nights, however, I have had to work well toward morning to get another sheet of experiments ready.

I remember telling you about ordering a lot of books, but I can not have told you of theirarrival just before college opened. The most useful things in the lot are the sets of the Botanische Zeitung and Pringsheim's Jahrbücher. The Annales des Sciences Naturelles does not come amiss either. For myself I rejoice chiefly in the copy of the Bryologia Europaea. THAT is just JOLLY, I tell you.

Only a few weeks ago the glass ware ordered for the physiological laboratory came to hand. With this and the few more important pieces of apparatus that I ordered, I feel that we have made a fair beginning toward a physiological laboratory. I believe it is the best, if not the only one, west of the Alleghanies.

My work on the mosses is progressing at the usual snail's pace. The packages are piling up faster than I can clear them off. Knowlton was out in the Yellowstone country all summer collecting fossil plants and brought in a stack of things with him, including two fat packages of mosses. Leiberg and Anderson continue to send me collections from Idaho and Montana respectively. I have packages on hands also from New Jersey, Kansas, Nebraska, California, and one on the way from Oregon. I believe I wrote you that Dr. Röll, the sphagnologist, (by the way you will remember him as the duffer whose paper on the classification of the Sphagnaceae you paged for me out of Flora---a mean job it was, for it had been reset) went on a collecting trip along the Northern Pacific in June last. He wrote me on his return, asking if I would elaborate a part of his collections, and came up from Chicago the other day to make final arrangements about the assignment. So there is that more to be done, and done by April 1. I am to do the Dicranaceae, Fissidenteae, Mniaceae and Polytrichaceae. Cardot, a French bryologist sent me 200 species of my desiderata the other day. This, together with

Mary continues to improve. She cannot use her eyes yet but is able to get around pretty vigorously. This will be fairly evident when I tell you that today she made three cakes,helped with the kitchen work a little,made a lot of small bows of ribbon for decorations, and went this afternoon to a History Club reading. (Doubtless you will wonder what under the sun we are going to do with THREE cakes! The wives and mothers of the resident members of the Beta Theta Pi fraternity are going to give the college chapter a house-warming Saturday night in honor of their occupancy of their new chapter house. Of which we are whom: hence the cakes and bows.)

Do not forget to tell me when you write how Mrs.Deane's health is now. When you last wrote she was not at all well. We hope that she has quite recovered. Mary joins me in warmest regards to her as well as yourself.

Write me also what you hear from Morong. When does Bailey intend returning and where is he going ?

If it is not too much trouble get me a little more of that lining in the bird's nest. I have a brilliant idea,and I'd like to see whether there is anything in it.

Remember me to all the Cambridge people when you see them--Goodale,Watson,Farlow,Seymour et al.

With warmest regards,ever faithfully yours,

Madison, Wis.
Dec. 22. 1888.

My dear Deane:—

For your Christmas gift I will write you a note in my own hand, to announce the sending of a small remembrance from my wife and myself to Mrs. Deane. We address it to her because it seems more appropriate, though we hope you too will enjoy the olives which it is meant to hold.

Please accept it

with our best wishes and sincerest regard.

I shall expect you to treasure your Xmas gift till next Xmas for I do not think you will get another till then. It feels too awkward and slow.

I am afraid that the small box will not get off till Monday and if it is a little late pardon our slowness. I have been too rushed to do anything about Xmas till today—

Ever faithfully yours,

C. R. Barnes

Madison, Wis., December 31. 1888.

My dear Deane:--

You seem to prize my handwriting so much that I feel almost guilty in writing you a letter with the Caligraph. But really you must excuse me this time. I have so much on hands just now and I can write so much faster on the machine, that I feel it to be a necessity to economize in the direction of time.

I meant to have acknowledged your kind remembrance that came on the same day that I took my delayed package to the office. The lectures I read shortly after they were first published, but I shall take great pleasure in re-reading them. Would that the hand that penned them had not lost its cunning. Speaking of this reminds me that I have lately got another picture of Dr. Gray. It forms one of a group of 25 botanists in attendance at the Manchester meeting of the B.A.A.S. The picture of the Doctor is excellent, though small, and it is pleasant to have it associated with those of such men as Treub, DeBary, Vines, Bower, Solms-Laubach, Saporta, Balfour, Pringsheim, Cohn, and many others whose names are known through their works. The picture is one that Arthur brought to me. I am also to have a set of his own photographs (4 x 5) of the interesting laboratories, botanic gardens, etc that he visited.

I enclose the letter from Mr. Morong. I was much interested in reading it. I hope he will be successful in his collecting.

I have had a busy time this -- vacation (?) in attending meetings of the various scientific, literary and educational bodies that select the holiday week and the capital for their meetings. I intended to use the vacation in preparing the paper that I am to read before the Literary Society in February(as you will see by the year book I send you.) But it has almost slipped away without my accomplishing anything.

I was surprised to hear that Bailey is back. I thought that he intended staying a year. But I guess there is hardly enough in Europe to occupy him a whole year.

The
Botanical Gazette.
EDITORS:
JOHN M. COULTER,
WABASH COLLEGE, CRAWFORDSVILLE, IND.
CHARLES R. BARNES,
UNIVERSITY OF WISCONSIN, MADISON, WIS.
J. C. ARTHUR,
PURDUE UNIVERSITY, LAFAYETTE, IND.

March 2. 1889.

My dear Deane:-

Morong's letter came from Bebb last night and I forward it at once with Bebb's which will explain why he delayed.

I greatly enjoyed the letter. Give M. my kindest regards & best wishes when you write –

I will try to get a letter written to you shortly. At this writing I am

Warmest regards to
Mrs. Deane –
Faithfully yrs,
G. R. Barnes

Madison, June 19

Dear Deane:- Don't think me entirely devoid of good feeling- It is the midst of our Commencement, which ends today & today I go out for a 3-days fishing tour. I will write you as soon as I come in- It's a shame that I did not do it long ago- Lay it on to my blamed procrastination & not intention to forsake you-

1877

Ever yours Barnes

NOTHING BUT THE ADDRESS TO BE ON THIS SIDE.

Walter Deane,
Cambridge,
Mass.

The
Botanical Gazette.

EDITORS:
JOHN M. COULTER,
WABASH COLLEGE, CRAWFORDSVILLE, IND.
CHARLES R. BARNES,
UNIVERSITY OF WISCONSIN, MADISON, WIS.
J. C. ARTHUR,
PURDUE UNIVERSITY, LAFAYETTE, IND.

June 27.1889.

My dear Deane:--

Well,I have been remiss,this time,haven't I ? Looking back over your letters I discover 5 since I wrote you a decent one. No one will be able to say that you are not longsuffering and patient with the derelict. If you know me as well as perhaps you think you do,you will know that there has been no deliberate intention to put aside the correspondence,but only (bad enough,in all conscience) a frequent postponement of a thing that was not pressing for one that was. I shall try not to be so slow hereafter.

Let me answer your question about the plant before I forget it. (This is the plant that Farwell sent you---has it been so long that you have forgotten it ?) It IS a moss---Fontinalis antipyretica,var. gigantea,Sulliv. It is of no especial interest,for it is quite common in just such situations as the collector found it in. His description of the shape of the leaves while in the water is especially good.

time it was discovered that it was falling from holes in the ceiling. As soon as that became evident the members of the faculty who were present organized themselves into "special police", a thing which happily we have nothing to do with ordinarily, with the intention of bagging the fellow who was pouring it through. He had put his head into the noose when he got up there, for there was only one normal mode of entrance or exit, and a search party was soon going thro the attic. In the mean time some of his confederates on the outside were captured and identified. When the fellow in the attic was finally about to be nabbed he took the desperate chance of kicking out a window and crawling along the edge of the roof till he could drop to the ground at a comparatively low place. He was nabbed however by the students below after a short chase and identified. We had lots of fun at the "inquest", tho it consumed the best part of three days. This was one of those rare cases in which the Faculty comes out on top. Having caught the principal actor and four of his pals, we felt pretty well satisfied as far as discipline can yield satisfaction. The chap who was caught in the attic was a senior engineer whose reputation had been of the best, and who had worked his own way thro. He was suspended indefinitely with the intimation that at some future time if his character and conduct were satisfactory he might receive his degree. The others got a year's suspension. The whole affair created quite a sensation in college and I guess got into the papers in a more or less exaggerated form.

ses were read, of which I send you a program. These are papers prepared by students whose standing has been very high in some special study, and who have devoted a large amount of time to this specialty. All are in English except the thesis in French, which is written in that language. In the afternoon came the class-day exercises. These are neither so extensive nor so sumptuous as those at Harvard. They consist of class song, prophecy, exhortation to the lower classes, etc., which are intended to be funny, and usually do keep the students and their friends who know the inside of the college life in a roar. This year in addition to the usual ceremonies the class had a funeral procession with the solemn burial of all the class records and other things. In the evening of the same day the class presented an original drama, written by one of their number. It was hugely ynjoyed by the largest audience of the season. It was full of good hits and take offs and was very cleverly presented.

On Tuesday the Alumni banquet was the chief feature. It differed in no respect from ordinary banquets. After the feed, came the speeches, some funny, some heavy; some wise, some otherwise.

Wednesday was the day when the graduates appeared in force. The speeches were considerably reduced in number this year; consequently these exercises were more enjoyable than usual, because they were not so exhausting. There were 12 speakers. I think they said there were about 160 in the class.

this year. We take along enough canned goods and bread to last us; sleep on the boat and get out for the early morning and late evening fishing, and rest through the middle of the day if the fishing is not so good as to tempt us to continue it. This year it was as bad as it could well be. Wednesday evening Owen and I each got a 4 lb. black bass, and Bunn two small yellow bass. Thursday was a capital fishing day, cloudy and finally rainy, with a good ripple on the water. Notwithstanding this only two fish were landed, a good yellow bass by Bunn and a small pickerel by Owen. Friday we were wind-bound. A tremendous blow from the N-W shook us up in our anchorage so that we were apprehensive of going ashore, while it entirely prevented any fishing. Late in the evening when the wind lulled a little we concluded to get out to a quieter shore. We were in a cove with a narrow channel and had to beat out. It took pretty hard work to get out of there with reefed sails, three boats in tow, water so shallow that we didn't dare give her more than 6 inches of centerboard, and a puffy wind that sometimes laid her cabin windows under and usually failed entirely just as we were ready to come about. By seven o'clock, however, we got to a new anchorage, in the lee of a high bluff, and made ready for the night. That is Trelease and I did, while Owen and Bunn went fishing. Owen came back with a black bass, Bunn empty handed. Saturday morning we tried our luck again, but it was as poor as ever. Trelease and I each got a 3-lb. pickerel; the others got---back. By noon we had had all the fishing we desired and put out for home. Good time---but no fish. Last year in August we got a good string---120 lbs. and over. We shall probably try it again after Owen gets back from the Rockies.

Of course we got lots of small fry---I should think as many as two hundred---rock-bass,roach,perch,white bass,etc.,but those don't count when you go for bigger game.

The summer school commences on the 9th of next month and continues till August 2nd. I have not yet heard what the prospect for students is,but suppose that we shall have between 50 and 60.

Trelease is going to spend the summer here. He is at work on Epilobium,and is just finishing a translation of a Danish Manual of Bacteriological Methods. He is doing that for the sake of learning the language. I enjoy his company mightily,I tell you. We went off a few days ago on a little collecting trip,and shall probably take a good many jaunts thro the summer. He wants to study up the water plants here. I wish you could be here with us. Can't you run out for a short time if you can't come for longer ?

We are in the pleasing condition of having no "girl" at present. Our maid was called home by telegram yesterday. We shall probably succeed in getting one before long however.

My wife wishes me to send her love to Mrs. Deane,with the hope that the New Hampshire air may hasten her recuperation. In these messages I join.

Ever yours faithfully,

C R Barnes

The
Botanical Gazette.
EDITORS:
JOHN M. COULTER,
WABASH COLLEGE, CRAWFORDSVILLE, IND.
CHARLES R. BARNES,
UNIVERSITY OF WISCONSIN, MADISON, WIS.
J. C. ARTHUR,
PURDUE UNIVERSITY, LAFAYETTE, IND.

Nov. 19. 1889.

My dear Deane:—

I received the letter conveying the sad news of the death of your father a day or two ago.

I remember with much pleasure meeting him and talking with him in his splendid library, and recall the enthusiasm he exhibited over some rare books. Had it been my good fortune to know him well, I am sure

pressed to me at Cambridge –

I lost my own father when I was so young that I never knew the pleasure of companionship between father and son in mature years, but I know it must be great and I feel deeply for you in your loss of it now.

My wife sends her regards and joins me in warm sympathy for your trial –

I shall try to send you an account of my doings soon –

Ever faithfully yrs. C. K. Burrill

The
Botanical Gazette.
EDITORS:
JOHN M. COULTER,
WABASH COLLEGE, CRAWFORDSVILLE, IND.
CHARLES R. BARNES,
UNIVERSITY OF WISCONSIN, MADISON, WIS.
J. C. ARTHUR,
PURDUE UNIVERSITY, LAFAYETTE, IND.

January 1st. 1890.

My dear Deane:--

You are certainly NOT out of my thoughts, though I have by my neglect given you reason perhaps to think so. I have been waiting ever since the vacation begun trying to get time to write you a MSS. A letter to accompany ~~your~~ my material remembrance, but something has always prevented. I thought I ought to write at least once a year in my own chirography, but I guess I shall have to put you off as I do my wife with a 'printed' letter. She takes them in default of better, and you must make the best of a bad bargain. It "tires" me so to write with a pen now: not mere muscular fatigue--rather mental, because I am all the time thinking how much quicker I could have written that word with a type-writer.

You call me facetiously and happily in your letter 'busy B.' You do not believe I know that I am half so busy as I think I am, nor one-quarter as much as I 'let on'. Well, may be I am not; but it as bad to think that you are overrun with occupations as to be actually so--perhaps wore. Since the 4th of last March when I began the examination of Böll's collection I have put all my spare time on that work. What spare time have I, do you ask ? Too little. I think you know that I am Superintendent of the Sunday School, which involves some work and often takes an evening. I have a standing engagement every Wednesday evening which I rarely fail to meet. Since the beginning of the college year in September I have had a standing engagement every Thursday evening. Dr Birge and I have been meeting our advanced students and reading with them Wallace's "Darwinism"--a course that had been both pleasant and profitable. We have but three chapters left. Saturday night we resume our readings of Shakespeare, which will give me a standing engagement every Saturday evening. Every second Monday of the month has been occupied with meetings of the Literary Club. Every third Monday with meetings of the Teacher's Association(S.S.). Every second Tuesday with meeting of the Monthly Musical Club. Every first Monday with meetings of the church session. Every Monday afternoon with meetings of the faculty. I have my mornings, barring numerous interruptions due to home and college work, for working at the mosses and unless I devote the time sacredly to them I get nothing at all accomplished. My afternoons until 4 are taken up with class work (12--1 & 2--4). In the good weather I gave from 4 to dark to tennis for exercise, and since that has been impossible I have put it in generally in study. Now in addition to this I have been giving from 2 to 3 days each month to work on the Gazette. Particularly since the first of November I have put in all the spare evenings in preparing the index. Well am I a "busy D."? I try not to keep myself in a stew about what I have to do, and I think I manage to get through it only by keeping steadily at it, with almost no deviation from a beaten track. Perhaps this outline of my work will give you as good an idea as anything of what I have been doing since I wrote you last. It is all a steady grind—tho' not unpleasantly so.

In the vacation (this Xmas) I spent two days at the meetings of the Wisconsin Academy of Sciences. The Sec'y 'boned' me for MSS. for the volume of the proceedings which is about going to press and as I was wanting a chance to print the keys to species of the larger genera of mosses which I have had in contemplation I said that I would undertake to furnish him copy in 30 days. I have finished and sent off the MSS. report on the Röll collection. I did a 'sight' of work there which will yield me little return in glory. I expected that I would find a considerable number of new species, but I found onle 3 new VARIETIES! I took my chances however! Now, I am putting in solid days on the preparation of those keys. If you have ever done anything of the kind you will know that it is not speedy work. I have finished all the genera containing over 5 species up to the genus Barbula on which

stay but a few minutes, as the constant cracking beneath my skates was too suggestive, altough there were numbers out, and even some ice boats were skimming around. The time so spent represented only the few minutes that I usually give to the Chicago paper after dinner.

Your paper knife perhaps looks fierce to an unaccustomed eye. If you could see the one that I had made for myself (since I could not buy what I wanted) you would think that yours was very inoffensive-looking. The blade of mine is just 12 inches long--long enough to cut the long side of a quarto at one fell swoop! (Have to have it so to save time!) It is steel, ground very thin, and flexible consequently, like a spatula.

Your letter of the 27th was quickly followed by the picture which I was delighted to see. You did not reckon wrongly in saying that I would like it. It will prove a constant delight as I look at it over my study table. I shall have it framed and hung in the library, where its distinguished faces will be a constant inspiration. I thank you warmly for the thoughtfulness which suggested sending for it for me.

I have been digging like a slave since Christmas at the keys to the larger genera of mosses, and am thankful to say that I have the job nearly completed. To construct the key to the genus Hypnum, with its 200 species, has been almost a herculean task. I have almost accomplished it, however, after a fashion, which I pray may prove better than my fears. Now I wish some one would undertake the Herculeo-Augean task of "cleaning out" the alleged species of the N.A. mosses. I think the shrinkage would amount to 10 or 12 per cent.

My wife came down with the influenza on Thursday and has been in bed with it ever since. She is progressing, however, and will be up tomorrow I hope. Otherwise the family is well.

Your humble servant has not time to extend his communication further today as he has a delightful engagement to meet at ten o'clock--- with a dentist. With warmest regards to Mrs. Deane,

Faithfully yours, C.R. Barnes.

The
Botanical Gazette.

EDITORS:
JOHN M. COULTER,
WABASH COLLEGE, CRAWFORDSVILLE, IND.
CHARLES R. BARNES,
UNIVERSITY OF WISCONSIN, MADISON, WIS.
J. C. ARTHUR,
PURDUE UNIVERSITY, LAFAYETTE, IND.

February 18.1890.

My dear Deane:--

Your various notes have coneto hand in due time and sequence and I have gladly spared the minute or two that it took to read them. Instead of rejoicing as you intimate that they are on small paper and <u>will</u> take but a minute to read I regret that you do not use larger sheets.

I have received also the printed slip with the names of the botanists in the picture, for which you have my thanks. I have attached it to my picture which is now framed and hanging in the library almost over my desk. Did I understand you that Dailey had it printed ?

I suppose it is to Dailey's ill health that I owe my immunity up to the present from an editorial slashing. When the Gazette noticed his bulletin on seed sprouting it had occasion to "rough" him a little on his slapdash style of work and publication. It inspired B. to write a letter to Coulter which expressed his amusement(?) at the ignorance etc.etc. of the critic. Coulter sent the letter to me and I replied to it; whereupon B. wrote a pleasant reply at the close of which he promised me an editorial roasting at an early day.

The
Botanical Gazette.
EDITORS:
JOHN M. COULTER,
WABASH COLLEGE, CRAWFORDSVILLE, IND.
CHARLES R. BARNES,
UNIVERSITY OF WISCONSIN, MADISON, WIS.
J. C. ARTHUR,
PURDUE UNIVERSITY, LAFAYETTE, IND.

March 11.1890.

My dear Deane:--

I am ashamed that your letter inquiring about the disposition of the Gray vase has been so long unanswered. I have really been too busy to do anything that could be put off, and have tonight my first breathing spell.

I have a very definite idea of what ought to be done with the vase, but I am uncertain whether it is practicable or not. In the first place I am quite convinced that the University in general ought not to have the vase. It has so much to look after already that this comparatively insignificant piece of property would soon sink out of sight, especially as soon as the circumstances of its gift are forgotten. Nor do I think that the Art Museum is the place for it. It is however my second choice. Here however is the is my ideal plan.

I think that Mrs Gray ought to leave the vase <u>specifically</u> to the <u>herbarium</u>, with the stipulation that it should be kept on exhibition there, either in the library or herbarium room. The only objection that I can see to this plan arises from the value of the vase (its intrinsic value) and the often unguarded condition of the rooms at the Herbarium. It seems ~~so that~~ however that provision could be made for these dangers. It ought to be possible to construct some sort of a case, with very heavy glass front that would allow the vase to be seen and at the same time protect it from sneak thieves. It seems to me perfectly certain-

C R Barnes

The
Botanical Gazette.
EDITORS:
JOHN M. COULTER,
WABASH COLLEGE, CRAWFORDSVILLE, IND.
CHARLES R. BARNES,
UNIVERSITY OF WISCONSIN, MADISON, WIS.
J. C. ARTHUR,
PURDUE UNIVERSITY, LAFAYETTE, IND.

July 23.1890.

My dear Deane:--

Well, I suppose that I have gotten my just deserts at
I have not heard from you for an age. I was flattering myself
had one correspondent that I might mistreat with impunity; that
one friend that would return good for evil. I give you cre it
ing it for a long time; for being far better to me tha my sins
omission deserved. I'm only sorry that you have not had the r
keep on heaping coals of fire on my head. It dawns on me now t
must have checked your kindness by that list of my increasing d
Was not that woful tale in the last letter that I wrote you ?

os supp]

plant ar

My letter was interrupted at this point and I resume it later.

I have great news for you now, but it is strictly confidential. I have just had a letter from Watson---saying---what do you think ? I am sure you never would guess it. He says that through the liberality of friends a sufficient income has been secured to warrant him in increasing the working force at the herbarium. He therefore wants ME (of all persons in the world) to come there and look after the mosses, rewrite the Field, Forest & Garden Botany and prepare a new Manual of mosses. I tell you it took my breath away almost. Of course I hae not given the proposition any serious consideration as yet, but I have the question staring me in the face now to decide. The matter of salary will of course cut some figure and I wish you would give me some data as to cost of living in Cambridge. What will a house of 7--9 rooms (depending on size) in a respectable part of Cambridge cost ? Will you tell me cost of fuel--hard coal--for range and furnace per ton. About how many tons do you use in a year ? These are the two largest items in the year's expenditure. The cost of provisions I can find in market reports, but these items are not quoted in any place accessible to me. If you will tell me about these I can form some estimate as to how much salary I shall be obliged to have.

Still later.

(This letter is something like those continued-in-our-next-dispatches that one sees in the city papers that issue a half-dozen editions daily. I shall conclude it this time.)

Of course just now I can hardly think of anything but the possibility of coming to Cambridge. You may well believe that the prospec of having all my time to work at the plants is a glittering one and tempts me strongly. If I can get a living salary I shall probably accept. But I am afraid that I can't live in Cambridge on less than $3000 without uncomfortable pinching. Give me your honest opinion on the subject --- and your experience if you will. We have n't any lux

October 9.1890.

My dear Deane:--

You are naturally curious I suppose to know what has become of my scheme as to coming to Cambridge,and I will take the first opportunity since the matter has been settled to enlighten you.

Not very much was done in the way of correspondence as I soon learned that Watson was going to do the unprecedented thing of coming to the meeting of the AAAS at Indianapolis. I therefore deferred all until I could talk with him face to face. On the Saturday excursion we had a chance to converse on the subject; a little more on the Monday excursion for the botanists and still more at Coulter's home at Crawfordsville,whither we both went for a couple of days after the meeting.

final decision as to my acceptance of the place. Last Monday I received an official notice from the Keeper of the Corporation Records ---the title smacks of royalty and compares favorably with 'the Keeper of the Robes' or 'the Lady of the Bedchamber'---that I had been appointed by the august body that he represents as an Assistant in the Herbarium for the year 1890--91. Good! I am therefore at the present time holding two large positions, and if I could only draw both salaries at the same time I would be reasonably happy. If everything goes well you may look for me in Cambridge on that most appropriate anniversary— All-Fool's Day; for ---was it not the great William who remarked ?---

'The wise man knows himself to be a fool.'

I think I wrote you that my wife had been ill most of the summer. She has gotten better now and is at her father's for a change of air and scene in the hopes of still further betterment. Her letters lead us to think that she is improving, and the new doctor whom she has consulted there says that he thinks she will come along all right. I am glad that she got away when she did for since she went we have had nothing but a succession of cloudy and rainy days, too warm for a fire and too cold and damp to be without one, a bad condition for neuralgia.

Let me hear from you, my dear fellow, whenever you get time. My warmest regards to Mrs. Deane.

Ever yours,

CRBarnes

The

Botanical Gazette.

EDITORS:
JOHN M. COULTER,
WABASH COLLEGE, CRAWFORDSVILLE, IND.
CHARLES R. BARNES,
UNIVERSITY OF WISCONSIN, MADISON, WIS.
J. C. ARTHUR,
PURDUE UNIVERSITY, LAFAYETTE, IND.

U. S Postal Guide, Jan. '91. p. 791.

§ 40. - By the act approved Jan. 24. 1888 the postage on seeds, cuttings, roots, scions and plants is at the rate of one cent for each two ounces or fraction thereof." (With Compliments of RL)

may 1891

NOTHING BUT THE ADDRESS TO BE ON THIS SIDE.

Walter Deane,
7 Brewster place,

The
Botanical Gazette.

EDITORS:
JOHN M. COULTER,
WABASH COLLEGE, CRAWFORDSVILLE, IND.
CHARLES R. BARNES,
UNIVERSITY OF WISCONSIN, MADISON, WIS.
J. C. ARTHUR,
PURDUE UNIVERSITY, LAFAYETTE, IND.

CAMBRIDGE, MASS.

July 16, 1891.

My dear Deane:--

Your note with its enclosed specimen reached me a day or two ago. The moss is Pogonatum urnigerum, not an uncommon species in mountainous regions. If you should keep your eyes open while prowling around such places you MIGHT find something that was not common. But I fear that there is little hope of you in the moss line!

We continue to hear favorable reports of my wife's condition, tho' the physician is unwilling to have her come away yet. I do not know what is best for her because I do not know how strong she is; so I am obliged to take her own and the doctor's reports. It may be that we shall conclude that it is not best for her to come on here; and it is possible that I shall go home earlier and take her to Madison. She is of course very homesick. Her sister has been visiting her recently and she is now expecting daily a cousin of whom she is very fond, so that she is not wholly without company. But withal she has the curious delusion that nobody quite fills the place of "somebody"! Queer, isn't it how some women are fooled ?

Everything is going on as usual at the Gardens. I think it is since you went away that Mrs. Gray filled the case in the library with Dr. G's writing materials and tools. Fernald returns from his vacation Monday. Dr. W's folks are away in the mountains and he keeps "bach."

With kindest regards to Mrs. Deane, in which mother joins, believe me,

Ever sincerely yours,

C. R. Barnes

The
Botanical Gazette.
EDITORS:
JOHN M. COULTER,
WABASH COLLEGE, CRAWFORDSVILLE, IND.
CHARLES R. BARNES,
UNIVERSITY OF WISCONSIN, MADISON, WIS.
J. C. ARTHUR,
PURDUE UNIVERSITY, LAFAYETTE, IND.

CAMBRIDGE, MASS,

July 24.1891.

My dear Deane:--

The little specimen that you send is the fructification of one of the Myxomycetes or slime moulds. In their vegetative condition they are naked masses of protoplasm which crawl about over and through rotting logs,damp soil,tan-bark,etc.by amoeboid movements. Sometimes these plasmodia (as the veg.stage is called) are as broad as one's 2 hands. One common species is canary yellow[illegible] and about the consistency of starch paste. When about to fruit they crawl up grass, twigs,etc.,lose a great part of their moisture and differentiate into the hard (relatively) skeletal parts which remain in this specimen, called the capillitium,and the spores. This one is a Stemonitis,probably fusca. It is common as slime moulds go,but few people see any of them,even the commonest.

I have just returned from an afternoon tea that Miss Newell gave to the botany-summer-schoolers,5--7. Miss N.asked the Ganongs,Mr.Dergen and us to stay to supper after the rest went and we had a charming evening because a congenial crowd.

Mary had another return of her neuralgia this month but was able wo write a long letter the next day. Formerly they used her up for several days. In spite of these backsets she has such strong assurances from outsiders as well as physicians and nurses that she is improving that we can hardly doubt it; indeed she recognizes it clearly. But she wants to get home and it is quite possible that we will go before long. I shall know in a week.----Fernald back,with loads of plants,mosses and other.---Miss Clark takes a week off next.--Dr.W.O.K.

Cordially, as ever, C.R.B.

The
Botanical Gazette.

EDITORS:
JOHN M. COULTER,
WABASH COLLEGE, CRAWFORDSVILLE, IND.
CHARLES R. BARNES,
UNIVERSITY OF WISCONSIN, MADISON, WIS.
J. C. ARTHUR,
PURDUE UNIVERSITY, LAFAYETTE, IND.

CAMBRIDGE, MASS.

July 31, 1891.

My dear Deane:--

I think thatI intimated in my last letter to you that we might decide to return to Madison sooner than I had intended when I last saw you. That decision has been reached and we leave here next Wednesday at 2:15. Mother and Lyle will go directly home, reaching Chicago at 4:50 the next afternoon. Leaving there at 6 they will reach M. at 10:25. I shall be with them as far as Battle Creek which we reach at 12:22. There I stop till the next day, and leaving on the same train reach home that evening at 10:25. The day will give me time to arrange everything for Mary without being hurried, and we get home at a comfortable time of night. From some Madison friends who stopped here on their way to Marblehead Neck I learned that our old servant was inquiring when we were expected in order that she might have the privilege (so she considers it) of putting the house in order for us and staying until a servant whom she has in mind for us can come. So we have written her and as she knows what and where every thing is we feel that things will be in good shape for us. She herself is to be married in Sept.

Addenda matter. I inserted the short ones with pen, and made a reference at the proper place to the long ones---"see p.735c".

Sorry that I shall not get to see you and Mrs. Deane again, but I expect to come on at Christmas.----Mary WENT TO A PICNIC Wednesday--by the doctor's orders! Took a drive out to Goguac Lake, 3 miles. Haven't heard what the result was. As ever, faithfully yours, C.R.B.

-THE-
Botanical Gazette.

EDITORS:
JOHN M. COULTER,
UNIVERSITY OF INDIANA, BLOOMINGTON, IND.
CHARLES R. BARNES,
UNIVERSITY OF WISCONSIN, MADISON, WIS.
J. C. ARTHUR,
PURDUE UNIVERSITY, LAFAYETTE, IND.

712 Langdon St., Madison, Wis.
December 8.1891.

My dear Deane:--

You really must pardon my seeming neglect. I truly thought the shoe was on the other foot and that I had written you a letter for which Iwas awaiting an answer.

Let me give you a brief history of the time since my last letter to you. We left Cambridge on the 5th of August,by the 'limited' over the Boston & Albany,which leaves Boston at 2:30 and arrives in Battle Creek at 12:20 the next day. Mother and Lyle went straight on,arriving in Madison at 10:25 in the evening. I found Mary anticipating my coming with the greatest impatience. She was at that time barely able to sit up for a short time and to walk the length of a not ample room. After seeing that her trunk was packed and a dozen other things attended to,I went down to the station,and as I thought engaged a berth on the next day's train. But when we got to the train the next day,the Wagner conductor assured me that the agent had not telegraphed or sent any other message calling for a berth; so that not only was there none made up as I had ordered but none was to be had. The train was full of "Grand Army" people returning early from the meeting at Detroit. I hesitated,but Mary was determined to get home at any cost so we went aboard. I got a full seat for Mary so that she could recline in the uncomfortable way that a day car permits. Fortunately this lasted only till we got to Kalamazoo,30 miles on,where another sleeper was put on. Then I had a berth made down and the rest of the journey was easy. We got home in the evening at 10:23. Mary was tired by the trip,but not nearly so much so as both she and I expected. Indeed getting home seemed to act like a tonic with her,and she began at once to improve. She had two recurrences of her pain,but has had none now for ~~over two~~ nearly three months and she begins to believe that the happy days the doctor prophesied when "there shall be no more pain" are truly coming. She has gained strength quite rapidly and is able to walk out now to the neighbors two blocks or more away. She is nearly if not quite back to her normal weight. Altogether I am quite satisfied that I did the best thing in bringing her home and feel that she is going to regain her former vigor.

For two months after we got home the house was in a "torn-up" condition. The cellar was cemented,furnace reset,a new mantel and hearth put in,the rooms all papered,the woodwork all varnished or refinished,the outside oiled and new storm-windows fitted. For a month we were without a 'girl'but have a good one now who is likely to be a fixture---for the winter at least. Mother has been working very hard,not only at the house settling,but for a fancy-work fair for the benefit of the new church. I have been "grinding" like Samson in the prison-house of the Philistines,trying to keep up with the demands on me in the determination of moss collections (which are almost hopelessly beyond me), in the revision of the F.F.& G.botany, as Secretary of the church building committee, as member of the State Board of Examiners (of teachers for licenses to teach), not to mention University duties (to which I am supposed to devote most of my time), editing (on the practical side) the GAZETTE, teaching a students class in S.S., and about a thousand and one other things to small singly to consider, but which in the aggregate nearly 'break the camel's back'.

Coulter and Arthur were up last week and spent two days with me on Gazette business. A.tells me that he is going to Cambridge (he wrote 'Boston', but I wot that through ignorance he did it; he surely means Cambridge) in the Christmas holidays. I hope that you will meet him. Have you, before ?

I had a very warm reception here on my return, and have not regretted that I came to the decision that I did, in spite of the tremendous attractions at Cambridge. I hoped that I would have so much done on the book that I would have to go to C.at Christmas, but I have made such poor progress that it will hardly pay! I jot down the things that I have to look up, and I shall have a host of them by June. I shall <u>have</u> to come then if not earlier.

We are glad to hear that Mrs.Deane improves and ho e that she may be strong enough before a great while to make that visit that you have so long deferred. My wife joins me in warmest regards to you both.

Most cordially yours, C.R.Barnes

THE
Botanical Gazette.

EDITORS:
JOHN M. COULTER,
UNIVERSITY OF INDIANA, BLOOMINGTON, IND.
CHARLES R. BARNES,
UNIVERSITY OF WISCONSIN, MADISON, WIS.
J. C. ARTHUR,
PURDUE UNIVERSITY, LAFAYETTE, IND.

712 Langdon St., Madison, Wis.

THE
Botanical Gazette.
EDITORS:
JOHN M. COULTER,
UNIVERSITY OF INDIANA, BLOOMINGTON, IND.
CHARLES R. BARNES,
UNIVERSITY OF WISCONSIN, MADISON, WIS.
J. C. ARTHUR,
PURDUE UNIVERSITY, LAFAYETTE, IND.

712 Langdon St., Madison, Wis.

Dec. 22. 1891.

My dear Deane:—

I sent by mail today a small remembrance, which I trust will reach you safe. With it go to you and your wife the warmest greetings à propos of the season. Would I could have given them in person.

When you unwrap the package don't think me a crank either as to wrapping or china! The numerous tunics are to avoid Uncle Sam's hard knocks.—But maybe I shall have to confess to a weakness for pretty dishes—At any rate I can't resist them! Most cordially yours, C.R. Barnes

THE
Botanical Gazette.
EDITORS:
JOHN M. COULTER,
UNIVERSITY OF INDIANA, BLOOMINGTON, IND.
CHARLES R. BARNES,
UNIVERSITY OF WISCONSIN, MADISON, WIS.
J. C. ARTHUR,
PURDUE UNIVERSITY, LAFAYETTE, IND.

712 Langdon St., Madison, Wis.

Jan. 4, 1892.

My dear Deane:-

Thank you very much for the pleasant book, so appropriate to the season, with which you remembered me on Christmas. Burroughs I enjoy very much. You sent me Fresh Fields, but Winter Sunshine I had not seen before. A note from Farlow tells me that you too have the grippe. I sincerely hope it is not so, but fear for you. As he says nothing of Mr. Watson I suppose he is out of danger.

Here's to you! Health, wealth and happiness for the New Year!

With my cordial greetings to Mrs. Deane, believe me,

Ever yours,

C. R. Barnes.

THE
Botanical Gazette.
EDITORS:
JOHN M. COULTER,
UNIVERSITY OF INDIANA, BLOOMINGTON, IND.
CHARLES R. BARNES,
UNIVERSITY OF WISCONSIN, MADISON, WIS.
J. C. ARTHUR,
PURDUE UNIVERSITY, LAFAYETTE, IND.

712 Langdon St., Madison, Wis.

January 5.1892.

My dear Deane:--

I embrace the first opportunity of the vacation to acknowledge the receipt of the book of Garner's on the speech of monkeys, and to thank you for the remembrance. I am particularly glad to have this book as it is one in which I am much interested from the accounts that I have read of his experimentation, and I shall take a great deal of pleasure in reading it.

All last week was devoted to the state examination of teachers fo certificates. Monday I went down to Chicago. I shall have the later days of this week to rest by catching up with correspondence which was entirely put aside last week.

I wish that you had been out here on the 26th. It would have given us much pleasure. A large number of our friends honored us with their presence on the occasion and seemed to enjoy themselves. A good many others were out of the city or had their own family reunions, so that the list of 'regrets' was large. A houseful o relatives also helped to make the week more or less festive, though I had little time after Monday to see anything of them.

Mary considers herself entirely well now. She has been through several rather trying "sieges" of either work or play, that a few months

THE
Botanical Gazette.
EDITORS:
JOHN M. COULTER,
UNIVERSITY OF INDIANA, BLOOMINGTON, IND.
CHARLES R. BARNES,
UNIVERSITY OF WISCONSIN, MADISON, WIS.
J. C. ARTHUR,
PURDUE UNIVERSITY, LAFAYETTE, IND.

712 Langdon St., Madison, Wis.

ago would have been impossible for her to stand without being entirely used up. She walks everywhere now, and has no trouble with here eyes except when she is very tired. She has seen lately one of the physicians and one of the nurses at the Sanitarium who knew her in her depression, and they are quite as much pleased with her progress as she herself. They bring reports as to the condition of some of the people whom we knew there, and whose cure is little short of marvellous. I have come to think very highly of the results that they achieve at Battle Creek--naturally.

I wish we might hear that Mrs. Deane was in good health again. We particularly want her to be able to come to Chicago next summer and come on to Madison to visit us. You must certainly plan to do it. For yourself the meeting of the botanists at Madison next summer will be of the greatest interest, and for her I am sure that the restfulness of our lake will be healthful.

My wife and mother join me in warmest regards to you both.

With the greetings of the season,

Ever yours,

C. R. Barnes

Madison, Wis. 23 F 92

My dear Deane:—

I await very anxiously further news from Dr. Watson. I know you will let me know when there is any change. I sincerely trust you may have good news to write. If you see any of the family convey to them my sympathy in their anxiety.

Wife about 50-50. Cordially, as ever Barnes.

POSTAL CARD ONE CENT.

United States of America.

MADISON, WIS.

THIS SIDE IS FOR ADDRESS ONLY.

Mr. Walter Deane,
Cambridge
Mass.

Madison, Wis., Mch. 25/92.

My dear Deane:—Will you take the trouble to select and send me the best cabinet photo of Dr. Watson obtainable? I want it for a half-tone portrait (like Anderson's in Mch) to accompany sketch. If there is any difference in prints select one with least deep shadows.—Thank you very much for sending such frequent bulletins. It was a great satisfaction.——Let me pay cost of photo.— Can you send it soon? Yrs ever Barnes

POSTAL CARD ONE CENT.

United States of America

THIS SIDE IS FOR ADDRESS ONLY.

12 M
189?

Walter Deane,

Cambridge,

9, Brewster pl. Mass.

THE
Botanical Gazette.
EDITORS:
JOHN M. COULTER,
UNIVERSITY OF INDIANA, BLOOMINGTON, IND.
CHARLES R. BARNES,
UNIVERSITY OF WISCONSIN, MADISON, WIS.
J. C. ARTHUR,
PURDUE UNIVERSITY, LAFAYETTE, IND.

712 Langdon St., Madison, Wis.

Apr. 11, 1892.

My dear Deane:—

The picture came duly to hand—and I thank you very much for taking the trouble to get it— It will probably be too much injured to be worth keeping— I send you herein 26¢ to pay for it— — Was much interested in your sketch of Dr. W. in the Apr. Torrey.— Still I am rushed— Kindest regards to Mrs. Deane—

Cordially, as ever,

C. R. Barnes

THE
Botanical Gazette.

EDITORS:
JOHN M. COULTER,
UNIVERSITY OF INDIANA, BLOOMINGTON, IND.
CHARLES R. BARNES,
UNIVERSITY OF WISCONSIN, MADISON, WIS.
J. C. ARTHUR,
PURDUE UNIVERSITY, LAFAYETTE, IND.

712 Langdon St., Madison, Wis.

October 21.1892.

My dear Deane:--

You have been shamefully neglected ,as,alas,you have been before; only this time I am not going to offer any explanation,beyond saying that it has been the old,old story of procrastination. You have been the friend who could be put off till the next time,and so you have been.

Your first postal came to me while I was at Rochester at the meeting of the AAAS. I really had some hopes of seeing you there,but you disappointed me. I want to tell you now that if you do not come to the great meeting next year at Madison I shall be obliged to drop you from my acquaintance. Seriously,you must begin to plan for it even now. We hope to have a cottage on our lake lot by next summer,and to spend a good part of the summer camping there. If that plan materializes we shall expect to have you and Mrs.Deane with us for a time. Then you can run down to the World's Fair,and come back for the meeting of the Association. We are really going to have a big meeting botanically speaking and you will miss it if you don't come.

We had a fine meeting at Rochester and did a good deal of important business. What we did in the matter of nomenclature is not in line exactly with Cambridge precedents but I believe that it is in line with the best practice of the botanists of the world (except Kew which simply says it will do its own way regardless of other people). However, anything is better than anarchy and I really think that we are now in a fair way to have another international agreement. If the U. S., Germany, France and Italy can agree on a common practice in the nomenclature of plants, Kew can go to grass. There is a good deal of work to be done in this line at the next meeting, for at the last we only made a start on a few general principles.

Aside from the business which the large and representative attendance rendered possible, it was a very pleasant meeting because so many of the men that one wants to meet were there. Next year we shall undoubtedly have a lot of the foreigners and most of our Pacific coast botanists. We take it for granted that all of the eastern fellows will be on hands.

As you have doubtless seen in the last Gazette I have given up the F.F.& G. work. It kept growing on my hands. The difficulties multiplied which I had foreseen in part. When I was working at Cambridge I told Mr. Watson that I feared it would be impossible to include all the plants that the plan contemplated; that the scheme of having only the commoner cultivated plants, which was practicable when Dr. Gray wrote the book, had become impracticable by reason of the rapid introduction of new plants in these days. Independently, Dr. Sargent expressed the same doubt, and by the time that I had finished the Leguminosae I had come to this conclusion. I intended to come to Cambridge last Christmas and talk the matter over with Dr. Watson, but his sickness prevented, and resulted so that consultation with him was impossible. When therefore Pres. Eliot wrote me to know how the book was progress-

THE
Botanical Gazette.
EDITORS:
JOHN M. COULTER,
UNIVERSITY OF INDIANA, BLOOMINGTON, IND.
CHARLES R. BARNES,
UNIVERSITY OF WISCONSIN, MADISON, WIS.
J. C. ARTHUR,
PURDUE UNIVERSITY, LAFAYETTE, IND.

712 Langdon St., Madison, Wis.

ing,I told him the condition of things,and said that I felt unable to produce a book that would be satisfactory to myself under the plan adopted,and was unwilling to put out work that I did not approve. He replied saying that they would much prefer that I go on with the work, but would like to know my wish in the matter frankly. I then wrote him asking to be relieved of the work and offering to give all the assistance in my power to whomever he should select to finish the job. At Rochester Bailey consulted me about it and then decided to accept the contract. I wish him joy of it. But he will do it much more easily than I could and without doubt much better. He is the man to whom it ought to have been given in the first place. I should never have thought of taking it had I not been flattered by the selection,and been almost certain that I should go to Cambridge. However I do not think that I made a mistake in declining and returning to Wisconsin.

Our new president has begun to get hold of the ropes and will do a good work for us I think. We felt quite broken up when Pres.Chamberlin decided to go to Chicago,but I think that Pres. Adams will do as much to counteract the ill effects of that as any one else could do. In spite of the uncertainties regarding the presidency,the opening of the new university of Chicago,and the raising of our entrance requirements a full half-year's work we have nearly 150 more students than last year. This will make our registration about 1250 this year. Owing to changes in the courses of study the biological department is overflowing. Dr.Birge and I have an elementary class of 130,with 2 lectures and 8 hours laboratory work a week. It takes 5 "hands" to

THE
Botanical Gazette.
EDITORS:
JOHN M. COULTER,
UNIVERSITY OF INDIANA, BLOOMINGTON, IND.
CHARLES R. BARNES,
UNIVERSITY OF WISCONSIN, MADISON, WIS.
J. C. ARTHUR,
PURDUE UNIVERSITY, LAFAYETTE, IND.

712 Langdon St., Madison, Wis.

run that class. In addition to that class I have an advanced class in general morphology. There is also a class of 20 in histology, which is under the charge of an assistant.

This winter we are talking of reading with our advanced students that new book of Romanes, Darwin and after Darwin.

My wife's health continues to improve. She is able to go about freely now and to take charge of the housekeeping again. The physician's prophecy came true in her case and she is now getting to feel like herself. I hope that Mrs. Deane got new strength from the summer at Jaffrey. How is she ?

My wife joins me in warmest regards, and adds her invitation to mine, that you come out next summer.

As ever, cordially yours,

C.R. Barnes

THE
Botanical Gazette.

712 Langdon St., Madison, Wis.

THE
BOTANICAL GAZETTE.
A monthly journal of botany.
Established in 1875.

$2.50
A YEAR.

EDITED AND PUBLISHED BY
JOHN M. COULTER
UNIVERSITY OF INDIANA, BLOOMINGTON.
CHARLES R. BARNES,
UNIVERSITY OF WISCONSIN, MADISON.
J. C. ARTHUR,
PURDUE UNIVERSITY, LAFAYETTE, INDIANA.

Madison, Wis., 23 D 1892

Dear Sir:

We beg to acknowledge with thanks the receipt of your late favor, with enclosure of $ 2.50 *covering* subs. 1893. —

(Book here. Many thanks. I shall enjoy reading it. — Sent you a photo yesterday of our park in winter. With warmest regards & the compliments of the season to you and Mrs. Deane, (Yrs ever Barnes)

Yours truly, THE BOTANICAL GAZETTE,

per CRB

POSTAL CARD ONE CENT.

United States of America

THIS SIDE IS FOR ADDRESS ONLY.

MADISON WIS.

Mr. Walter Deane,
9 Brewster st.,
Cambridge,
Mass

THE
Botanical Gazette.
EDITORS:
JOHN M. COULTER,
UNIVERSITY OF INDIANA, BLOOMINGTON, IND.
CHARLES R. BARNES,
UNIVERSITY OF WISCONSIN, MADISON, WIS.
J. C. ARTHUR,
PURDUE UNIVERSITY, LAFAYETTE, IND.

Dictated

712 Langdon St., Madison, Wis.
Apr. 10, 1893.

My dear Dean:—

Your two letters, as usual, have gone unanswered for a long time. I am always glad to hear from you, and I would write more promptly if I did not have so many other letters, that ~~could~~ can not be put off, to attend to. I have been practically forced into taking up the arrangements for the coming meeting here of the A.A.A.S. I am the Local Secretary, and have a good deal of the executive work to do. That, with the Gazette, University, and church duties, is going to keep me swamped for another three months.

I suppose you are coming out this way sometime during the summer. I hope very much that Mrs. Dean will be able to travel, and if you do come this way, we shall anticipate having both of you visit with us, but even if she is not able to come, certainly you will break away this time and see not only the Fair but the A.A.A.S. You know we are going to try to have a big Botanical Congress, or at least an important one, and I am sure you will never have an opportunity again to meet so many botanists as you will have this summer; but I think we planned out all of this sometime ago, and if I mistake not I have your consent to come.

My wife continues to improve in health, and is about to start to make a visit at her home. He father's health is not good; indeed he

THE
Botanical Gazette.
EDITORS:
JOHN M. COULTER,
UNIVERSITY OF INDIANA, BLOOMINGTON, IND.
CHARLES R. BARNES,
UNIVERSITY OF WISCONSIN, MADISON, WIS.
J. C. ARTHUR,
PURDUE UNIVERSITY, LAFAYETTE, IND.

712 Langdon St., Madison, Wis.

is confined to his bed at present, and I think it is very doubtful whether he ever gets up, although he is in no immediate danger. He suffered several years ago a stroke of paralysis, and the defective circulation induced by that has brought on a disease in the foot similar to gangrene, which may finally result in his death, although it is possible that he will recover from it. The boy keeps well, and is going to the kindergarten, beginning to read, and in general 'getting a big boy.'

Did you know that Coulter was about to change his location again? He has been elected President of Lake Forest University near Chicago, and will be considerably nearer to me. Indiana University came to be rather hopeless when the Legislature sliced its desired appropriation in half, and as Bloomington is not a particularly desirable place in which to live, John concluded he would come to a place where he might have "creature comforts" at least for his family, as well as a considerably increased salary for himself. Lake Forest is considered ~~a~~ the most beautiful suburb of Chicago, and Presbyterians of that city are likely to be stimulated into giving some of their millions to developing this already flourishing Presbyterian institution.

Give our kindest regards to Mrs. Deane, and say to her that we are

THE
Botanical Gazette.
EDITORS:
JOHN M. COULTER,
UNIVERSITY OF INDIANA, BLOOMINGTON, IND.
CHARLES R. BARNES,
UNIVERSITY OF WISCONSIN, MADISON, WIS.
J. C. ARTHUR,
PURDUE UNIVERSITY, LAFAYETTE, IND.

712 Langdon St., Madison, Wis.

greatly pleased to hear that she is so much improved in health. We hope that she will be sufficiently well this summer to take the long journey westward which separates us.

With warmest regards,

Yours sincerely C.R. Barnes

Mr. Walter Deane,
9 Brewster Place,
Cambridge, Mass.

THE
Botanical Gazette.
EDITORS:
JOHN M. COULTER,
UNIVERSITY OF INDIANA, BLOOMINGTON, IND.
CHARLES R. BARNES,
UNIVERSITY OF WISCONSIN, MADISON, WIS.
J. C. ARTHUR,
PURDUE UNIVERSITY, LAFAYETTE, IND.

712 Langdon St., Madison, Wis.

May 3, 1893.

My dear Deane:-

I find your letter of the 27th awaiting me. It will give me great pleasure to send Dr. Gray's letter to Mrs. Gray, and I will do so immediately.

I also have your letter expressing doubt as to your ability to come west this summer. I regret very much that y u think it even doubtful, for I had hoped that Mrs. Deane would be quite able to travel this summer. She ought at least to let you off long enough to come alone, and I think I shall have to send her a personal appeal to that effect.

Very truly yours

C.R. Barnes

Mr. Walter Deane,
9 Brewster St.,
Cambridge, Mass.

EW.

THE
Botanical Gazette.

712 Langdon St., Madison, Wis.
May 13, 1893.

My dear Deane:-

I am very sorry that I overlooked a call for extras of your recent note in the Gazette. Was this request entered upon the manuscript, or was it made in some subsequent communication? I can hardly believe that I overlooked such a memorandum upon a manuscript, although of course I may have done so. I take pains to go over each one, looking for just this thing. If it was not upon the manuscript I shall not feel so bad about my oversight, because that is the only place where I would be sure of seeing it at the right time, and it is the place where the authors are directed to indicate their desire for separates. If you are sure that the order was on the manuscript, we will re-set the article, and print extras without additional expense. None were printed at the proper time.

Very truly yours

C. R. Barnes.

Mr. Walter Deane,
Cambridge, Mass.

UNIVERSITY OF WISCONSIN.

MADISON, WIS., U. S. A.

DEPARTMENT OF BOTANY.
C. R. BARNES.
PROFESSOR OF BOTANY.

Dec. 25. 1893.

My dear Deane:-

The beautiful penknife which you were so thoughtful as to send came to hand in season for the day. I assure you I appreciate it very much and shall find it a pleasure to carry a token which will remind me of you every time I have occasion to take it from my pocket.

Last Friday I mailed you a book by one of our local literati which I think you will find interesting not only on account of the charming literary style but also for its flavor of outdoor life and particularly its connection with what seems to have become your favorite amusement. Mr. Thwaites is secretary of our historical society whose library is counted one of the finest in the country. His own contributions in the field of early history of the Northwest were doubtless well known to your father if not to you.

I enjoyed an evening with our mutual friend, Judge Churchill when he was here in August and had the pleasure of entertaining him & Mrs. Churchill at tea. Have had a letter from him since, speaking of his enjoyment in looking over again the plants he collected here and at Chicago.

I am pleased to be able to give you a good account of Mary's health. She has constantly grown stronger and now does full duty in the household and outside, though she has to be a little careful about too much walking yet. But I regret to say that mother has had a very serious illness from which she is only now recovering very slowly. She has been in bed nearly three months, being prostrated in October with a hemorrhage of the stomach produced by ulceration of its mucous membrane. This comes about as a sequela of chronic dyspepsia. The Dr. told us at the outset that the outcome would be long delayed, whether it was recovery or the reverse. For weeks she was in imminent danger, since there was no way of knowing whether the ulceration would cicatrize or continue to destroy the tissues until perforation ensued. I think now that he considers her nearly out of danger. She sits up a couple of hours a day now and is eating solids again. But she gains strength very slowly and it will be some time yet before she can get up and be dressed. We have had a trained nurse most of the time for her. Mary had just gone thro' a siege of 6 weeks nursing her sister who was ill here in the early autumn and after two weeks with mother gave out. Fortunately we have had efficient help in the kitchen all the time.

Some happy day I hope we shall all be well at once! — Give our warmest regards to Mrs. Deane, whom you may also congratulate for us on her regained health.

Ever fraternally yours, C.R. Barnes

ESTABLISHED 1879 THE PER ANNUM $3.00

BOTANICAL GAZETTE

A MONTHLY JOURNAL OF BOTANY, EDITED AND PUBLISHED BY

JOHN MERLE COULTER : CHARLES REID BARNES : JOSEPH CHARLES ARTHUR

DEAR SIR: MADISON, WIS. 19 7 94

We beg to acknowledge with thanks the receipt of your late favor with enclosure of MS. on Ware collection, which will be published as soon as possible. Separates will be furnished as ordered. Please send copy for cover.

Yours truly,

THE BOTANICAL GAZETTE.

Per C.R.B.

POSTAL CARD ONE CENT.

United States of America

THIS SIDE IS FOR ADDRESS ONLY.

M
1894

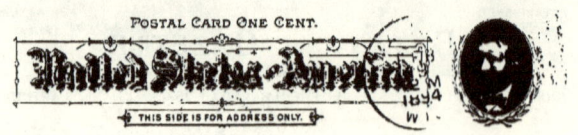

Walter Deane, Esq.
9 Brewster st.
Cambridge
Mass.

THE BOTANICAL GAZETTE

JOHN MERLE COULTER : CHARLES REID BARNES : JOSEPH CHARLES ARTHUR

Dear Sir :

We should consider it a favor if you would notify us promptly of any errors, typographical or other, occurring in your article in the last number of the **Botanical Gazette,** *in order that they may be corrected at the close of the volume.*

Yours truly,

THE BOTANICAL GAZETTE,

Madison, Wis.

Separates in a day or two
CRB

POSTAL CARD ONE CENT.

United States of America

THIS SIDE IS FOR ADDRESS ONLY

12 M
1894
W 10

Walter Deane
Cambridge
Mass.

My dear D:— Your note is welcome. Sorry to say you are too late for more reprints as type is all "thrown in"—

Yours ORB

16 Ap 94.

THE
Botanical Gazette.
EDITORS:
JOHN M. COULTER,
LAKE FOREST UNIVERSITY, LAKE FOREST, ILLS.
CHARLES R. BARNES,
UNIVERSITY OF WISCONSIN, MADISON, WIS.
J. C. ARTHUR,
PURDUE UNIVERSITY, LAFAYETTE, IND.

OFFICE OF PUBLICATION,
MADISON, WIS.

May 2. 1894.

My dear Deane:-

Your card and letter rec'd. I am very sorry to hear of Dr. Morong's death. Will you not prepare a biographical sketch of him for the ~~[illegible]~~ June no.? Get copy here by 25th inst. at latest if you will. Say 800–1200 words. Let me hear.

Hastily
C.R.B.

ESTABLISHED 1879

THE

BOTANICAL GAZETTE

PER ANNUM $3.00

A MONTHLY JOURNAL OF BOTANY, EDITED AND PUBLISHED BY

JOHN MERLE COULTER : CHARLES REID BARNES : JOSEPH CHARLES ARTHUR

DEAR SIR:

MADISON, WIS. 4 My 94

We beg to acknowledge with thanks the receipt of your late favor with enclosure of $1.50 for separates Apl. no.

Yours truly,

THE BOTANICAL GAZETTE.

Per CRB

POSTAL CARD ONE CENT.

United States of America

THIS SIDE IS FOR ADDRESS ONLY.

SON,
6 PM
94

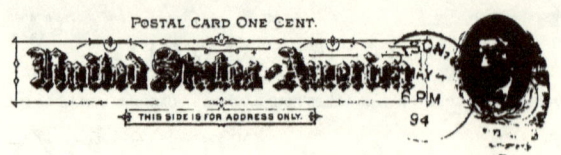

Mr. Walter Deane –
9 Brewster st.
Cambridge
Mass

ESTABLISHED 1879 | THE | PER ANNUM

BOTANICAL GAZETTE

A MONTHLY JOURNAL OF BOTANY, EDITED AND PUBLISHED BY

JOHN MERLE COULTER : CHARLES REID BARNES : JOSEPH CHARLES ARTHUR

DEAR SIR: MADISON, WIS. 6 Jy 94

We beg to acknowledge with thanks the receipt of your late favor with enclosure of $1.00 for separates Bot. Gaz.

My dear Deane:– I shall try to write you soon. We are out at summer cottage now & I only get in for a short time daily on my wheel! Sketch of Morong is good & Argentina is OK

Yours truly,

THE BOTANICAL GAZETTE.

Per ____

POSTAL CARD ONE CENT.

United States of America

THIS SIDE IS FOR ADDRESS ONLY.

MADISON

Walter Deane

The Arundel ~~Cambridge~~

Kennebunkport

~~Mass.~~

Me.

~~4 Brewster~~ ~~pl.~~

THE
Botanical Gazette.
EDITORS:
JOHN M. COULTER, LAKE FOREST UNIVERSITY, LAKE FOREST, ILL.
CHARLES R. BARNES, UNIVERSITY OF WISCONSIN, MADISON, WIS.
J. C. ARTHUR, PURDUE UNIVERSITY, LAFAYETTE, IND.

OFFICE OF PUBLICATION,
MADISON, WIS.

October 16, 1894.

My dear Deane:--

I have your letter of the 7th inquiring about the publication of a notice of Bailey's Note Book. Generally the notices of books published in the Gazette are written by the editors, and on all cases when this is not so, they are signed by the author. I wonder that B. has not sent the Gazette a copy of his book, as he is quite aware of its existence and standing. I believe that all the notices which have been written by others than the editors have been about books which it could hardly be expected the editors should receive, but I cannot say positively. However we should be glad to be relieved of the work of preparing a notice in this case, and if you will kindly send me a copy, or ask Bailey to do so, we shall gladly take your MS. If you send yours of course I should return it.

I do not know whether you know or not that we have been building a new house this summer; we have just moved into it, and are settled enough to live comfortably. But it is not completed yet, since two mantels and the book cases are yet to be set. The mantels I designed myself, and as I was rather slow in placing the order they were not done as soon as they ought to have been. I wish you could visit us in our own home, an we will hope that you may. If Mrs. Deane is able to walk so far now, surely she will be able to travel, and you will be coming to Chicago some day to see your brother; then you can run up and see us. Of course we think the house is pretty. I will send you some photographs of it as soon as the leaves get off the trees, when I hope to have some views of the exterior, and at the same time of the interior. The interior has not been dressed up yet, so that we can hardly tell what it will look like. Draperies are as necessary to a house as to a woman, though in both cases they are a nuisance from the practical point of view.

You have no idea, unless you have built a house, how many details there are to be looked after, and how much time it takes to see that "all things work together for good". I was helping mother, too, a good part of the time in getting the summer cottage that she built this spring into shape. We occupied it a good part of the summer, and there was clearing up the woodland about it, putting in the hooks, shelves and innumerable fixtures necessary for comfort and ornament, to do. The 4 weeks summer school and a week of teachers examinations for state certificates took my time for July. About the middle of August I got away for 10 days to the Brooklyn meeting A.A.A.S.---So you see that I have not been idle.

Mary is quite well, though she had a cold last week that made her 'pretty miserable, thank you' for a few days. Her sister has come to live in Madison, with her three children, and in addition to getting our own house settled she has done a tremendous amount of work in helping her sister get her house in order. You know the indefinitely numerous

THE
Botanical Gazette.

OFFICE OF PUBLICATION,
MADISON, WIS.

trips for shopping that are necessary under such conditions. If you don't I am sure that Mrs. Deane will.

I've been meaning to tell you about that Argentina business about which you asked me. Argentina is all straight in spite of Lippincott. That is the official name of the country, and it so appears in the latest German atlases. Therefore I let it stand. Only today I was in the capitol, when the Superintendent of Public Property said to me, "I have a couple of packages from Argentina which belong to the Academy". And that is probably what made me think of it again.

I am glad that you found such pleasure in the little book. I think Mr. Thwaites has a most happy style. You would enjoy his "Historic Waterways", the account of a canoe trip down the Wisconsin and Fox rivers. This summer he and Mrs. T. took a similar trip down the Ohio from Pittsburg to Cairo.

Mary joins me in kindest regards to yourself and Mrs. Deane, as also does mother. She, I am sorry to say, does not get back to her usual health since the severe illness last winter, but she is able to be about and to occupy herself with study and reading. Do not be afraid that we shall ever forget you, or be willing to let the ties of friendship loosen. We have too much in common and received too many kindnesses from you at Cambridge ever to do that.

Yours faithfully,

C. R. Barnes

THE

Botanical Gazette.

EDITORS:
JOHN M. COULTER,
LAKE FOREST UNIVERSITY, LAKE FOREST, ILLS.
CHARLES R. BARNES,
UNIVERSITY OF WISCONSIN, MADISON, WIS.
J. C. ARTHUR,
PURDUE UNIVERSITY, LAFAYETTE, IND.

OFFICE OF PUBLICATION,
MADISON, WIS.

ESTABLISHED 1879 | THE | PER ANNUM $3.00

BOTANICAL GAZETTE

A MONTHLY JOURNAL OF BOTANY, EDITED AND PUBLISHED BY

JOHN MERLE COULTER : CHARLES REID BARNES : JOSEPH CHARLES ARTHUR

DEAR SIR: MADISON, WIS. 21 N. 94.

We beg to acknowledge with thanks the receipt of your late favor with enclosure of MS. We hope that you will send a series under the same title. ~~If so~~ we will number this I, & will publish it early next year (prob. Jan. no.) Yours truly,

THE BOTANICAL GAZETTE.

Per C.R.B.

POSTAL CARD ONE CENT.

United States of America

THIS SIDE IS FOR ADDRESS ONLY.

Mr. Walter Deane
9 Brewster st.
Cambridge Mass.

ESTABLISHED 1879 THE BOTANICAL GAZETTE PER ANNUM $3.00

A MONTHLY JOURNAL OF BOTANY, EDITED AND PUBLISHED BY

JOHN MERLE COULTER : CHARLES REID BARNES : JOSEPH CHARLES ARTHUR

MADISON WIS. 25 O 94.

DEAR SIR:

We beg to acknowledge with thanks the receipt of your late favor with ~~enclosure of~~ accompanying book. Bailey has just sent a copy & yours is returned herewith.

Yours truly,

THE BOTANICAL GAZETTE.
Per C.R.B.

POSTAL CARD ONE CENT.

United States of America

THIS SIDE IS FOR ADDRESS ONLY.

MASS. OCT 2[illegible] 12 M 94

CAMBRIDGE STA. OCT 2[illegible]

Mr. Walter Deane
9 Brewster st,
Cambridge
Mass.

THE
Botanical Gazette.
EDITORS:
JOHN M. COULTER, LAKE FOREST UNIVERSITY, LAKE FOREST, ILL.
CHARLES R. BARNES, UNIVERSITY OF WISCONSIN, MADISON, WIS.
J. C. ARTHUR, PURDUE UNIVERSITY, LAFAYETTE, IND.

OFFICE OF PUBLICATION,
MADISON, WIS.

Jan. 7. 1895.

My dear Deane:—

The holidays are over and I have not even acknowledged your very acceptable gift which came the day before Christmas! But I am sure you have got so used to my sins of omission that one more will not turn you against me. So forgive until seventy times seven at least. "Riverby", from the dips I have taken into it, quite equals Burroughs's other charming collections of out door sketches and I shall enjoy it as I did "Fresh Fields" and "Winter Sunshine". Thank you for the thought and thank you for the <u>thoughts</u>.

When you get time send me a little additional material for your Notes II. The installment is rather too short. No hurry; we shall probably not get to it before March at earliest.

All well.— I shall send you photo of new house as soon as I can get time to [illegible] it properly. — Term opened today, Our attendance will reach about 1500. — Governor Upham (Rep) inaugurated today & great Inaugural Ball now in progress at U. W. Gymnasium, where the unobstructed floor 176 x 176 has been canvassed! What a place to dance! Eh?

Kindest regards to Mrs. Deane. We are so glad that she can again enjoy doing what she wants to do without considering a back! We (Mary & I) spent 3 days in Chicago last week, going to Univ. Convocation at Auditorium to hear Seth Low speak & spending all next day on foot going over Univ. buildings, the Field Columbian Museum etc.; then shopping; all this she stood with quite as little fatigue, I think, as I, though I am said to be in prime physical condition. She adds, she is too! Good.

Now begin to plan to come west next summer. Mrs. D. has no longer any excuse, much less a reason.

But time fails with pen. Come & I'll talk it over with you —

Yours ever Barnes

THE

Botanical Gazette.

EDITORS:

JOHN M. COULTER,
LAKE FOREST UNIVERSITY, LAKE FOREST, ILLS.

CHARLES R. BARNES,
UNIVERSITY OF WISCONSIN, MADISON, WIS.

J. C. ARTHUR,
PURDUE UNIVERSITY, LAFAYETTE, IND.

OFFICE OF PUBLICATION,
MADISON, WIS.

January 19.1895.

My dear Deane:--

I have your letter of the 14th enclosing additional matter for your notes II. About the illustrations: I am afraid that the plates will cost too much for our pocket-book. Those half-tone plates cost us about $9 apiece and $3 for printing. That would make the bill for five $60. We should greatly like to illustrate the series of seedlings of the Pontederia, and also your Utricularias. Could you not combine the Pontederias somehow and get some of your friends to make outline sketches of them which we could photo-engrave ? Send me the prints and let me see what can be done with them.

I had no copy of Riverby before yours came. I should have obeyed your first injunction had I possessed a copy.

The next issue of the Gazette containing an installment of your notes will have a brief account of your herbarium and the grounds of your confidence!

I hardly dare send MS. with proof for fear proof will be lost or so delayed that the article will have to be corrected by us by MS. and so issued.

The Botanical Gazette A Monthly Journal of Botany: Edited and published by John Merle Coulter, Charles Reid Barnes, Joseph Charles Arthur. Established 1875. Subscription, $3.00 a year.

Madison, Wis. 23 7 189*5*

DEAR SIR:

We beg to acknowledge with thanks the receipt of your late favor, with enclosure of Notes & the photos

Will write you soon. Crowded now!

Yours truly,

^

POSTAL CARD - ONE CENT.

United States of America.

THIS SIDE IS FOR THE ADDRESS ONLY.

5 P
95

Mr. W. Deane
9 Brewster st.
Cambridge Mass

The Botanical Gazette: A Monthly Journal of Botany: Edited and published by John Merle Coulter, Lake Forest University, Lake Forest, Illinois; Charles Reid Barnes, University of Wisconsin, Madison, Wisconsin; and Joseph Charles Arthur, Purdue University, Lafayette, Indiana. + + Established 1875. + + Subscription $3.00 a year.

OFFICE OF PUBLICATION, 616 LAKE ST., MADISON, WIS.

March 5. 1895.

My dear Deane:--

I have been away from home so much in the past few weeks that my correspondence, even business, has got far behind. I take up the two letters of yours which I find on my desk unanswered.

It is not a difficult problem that you propound as to the change of letters in your separates, and not in the Gazette sheets. In transferring the forms to the smaller press for printing the separates the two letters fell out. The pressman then proceeded to stick them in where it was most convenient, and through the inherent cussedness of inanimate objects he got them in just the wrong places.

As to the photographs, which I return to you by this mail: I hardly know what to say. They are beauties, and the specimens they represent are the same. I wish we could reproduce them, for I think they would be a pattern, not to say a stimulus for collectors. But---there is always a b u t, a fly in the pot of ointment---each one of them will take a whole plate, and that means about $13 to us, which is simply out of the question. We are willing to illustrate abundantly, but $00 to $130 is too much to put into either patterns or stimuli! And I know no way in which these photographs can be reproduced cheaper.

Of course if you have some extra cash that you want to blow in we'd be pleased to do the printing for you! For instance: you furnish the blocks and we'll print the plates, which costs us $3 each.

I hope to get another installment of your Notes in the April number. March was filled up with stuff that has been hanging fire so long it was losing its freshness and I had to run it in.

Cordially yours,

CRBarnes

Underwood's prints are far better than the other man's. B.

MAR 23 1895

My dear Deane:- I send you today the long-promised photos of our house. The exterior view is taken looking to the N.W., showing the lake. The interior shows a part of the Liby. All well. How are you. — Your notes are to be cont'd in Apr. no.-

Yours as ever

Barnes

POSTAL CARD - ONE CENT

United States of America.

THIS SIDE IS FOR THE ADDRESS ONLY.

MADISON MAR 23 5 PM

Mr. Walter Deane

Cambridge

9 Brewster st. Mass.

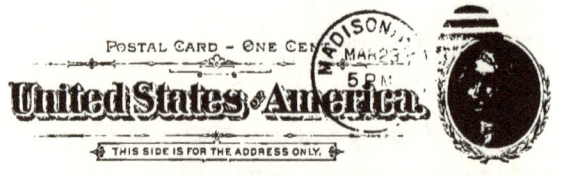

The Botanical Gazette A Monthly Journal of Botany: Edited and published by John Merle Coulter, Charles Reid Barnes, Joseph Charles Arthur. Established 1875. Subscription, $3.00 a year.

Madison, Wis. MAR 25 1895 *189*

DEAR SIR:

We beg to acknowledge with thanks the receipt of your late favor, with enclosure of MS. — Notes III. Order for Extras noted. —— Will make text out of glue pot.

Yours truly,

THE BOTANICAL GAZETTE.

Per Barnes

POSTAL CARD - ONE CENT.

United States of America.

THIS SIDE IS FOR THE ADDRESS ONLY.

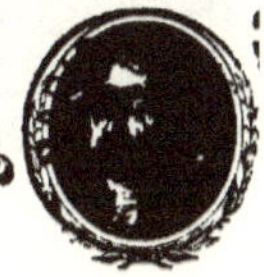

Walter Deane-

Cambridge

9 Brewster St. Mass

The Botanical Gazette: A Monthly Journal of Botany: Edited and published by John Merle Coulter, Lake Forest University, Lake Forest, Illinois; Charles Reid Barnes, University of Wisconsin, Madison, Wisconsin; and Joseph Charles Arthur, Purdue University, Lafayette, Indiana. + + Established 1875. + + Subscription $3.00 a year.

OFFICE OF PUBLICATION, 616 LAKE ST., MADISON, WIS.

MAY 10 189.

Dear Deane:– Your p.c. & remittance at hand. Thank you – As to cost of separates: Our contract with printers is so much per 4 pp. <u>or less</u>. It costs just as much to do presswork on 1 page as on 4, and it is presswork that costs, the item of paper in such small editions being inconspicuous. That means that it is as much trouble and takes as much time to prepare form for the job press, do the printing & clean the type, for 1 pp. as for 4 pp. And if one line only stays on a page it has to be run. On each 4 pp. we charge you 10¢ over cost to us to cover wrapping & postage. The 25 free are <u>wholly</u> free. As to two lots: the fact is the printer charged us just the same for the two, but as first was really only 4 pp. of type we chgd you for only 4 pp. while we paid for 8. The reason for this was that as your article commenced on an "even" page (12) the preceding page of the separate form had to be blank, which costs just as much in printing as tho' it were full of type! That is the printer's "fat". But as you were not responsible for its commencing on an even page we stood the loss. Had we been able to arrange it to begin on an "odd" page we should have had to pay for only 4 pp.

All well. Are you planning to be at Springfield at the A.A.A.S.? If you don't I shall cut your scientific acquaintance!

Cordially, as ever,

C.R. Barnes

My dear Deane:— The moss you sent May 25th was not Dichelyma pallescens but D. capillaceum. I could not get at it sooner. Commencement ~~next~~ next week — then a breathing spell.

FROM
C. R. BARNES
MADISON, WIS.

Yours as ever
C.R.B.

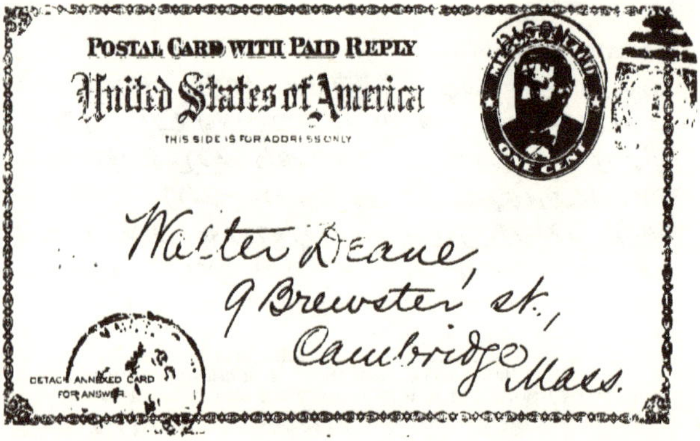
POSTAL CARD WITH PAID REPLY
United States of America
THIS SIDE IS FOR ADDRESS ONLY
Walter Deane,
9 Brewster st.,
Cambridge Mass.
DETACH ANNEXED CARD FOR ANSWER.
ONE CENT

The Botanical Gazette A Monthly Journal of Botany: Edited and published by John Merle Coulter, Charles Reid Barnes, Joseph Charles Arthur. Established 1875. Subscription, $3.00 a year.

Madison, Wis. JUN 21 1895 189

DEAR SIR:

We beg to acknowledge with thanks the receipt of your late favor, with enclosure of MS. which we shall use as early as possible. No III will come in Aug. We are making a convenience of these notes you see. So crowded lately that we had to put them over for others that would spoil by keeping.

Yours truly,

THE BOTANICAL GAZETTE.

POSTAL CARD - ONE CENT.

United States of America

THIS SIDE IS FOR THE ADDRESS ONLY.

MADISO[N] JUN 5 PM 95

Mr. Walter Deane
9 Brewster st.
Cambridge
Mass.

The Botanical Gazette A Monthly Journal of Botany: Edited and published by John Merle Coulter, Charles Reid Barnes, Joseph Charles Arthur. Established 1875. Subscription, $3.00 a year.

Madison, Wis. AUG 20 1895 189 .

DEAR SIR:

We beg to acknowledge with thanks the receipt of your late favor, ~~with enclosure of~~ The plates, we regret to say, did not reach this office until too late to get into the proper number. They will be sent out with the Dept. no. Your separates will be sent shortly now. Have been waiting for plates. Notes III separates went to Cambridge — Heisel sent 600 he says. Will let plates you know.

Yours truly,

THE BOTANICAL GAZETTE.

Per C.R.B.

P.S. I leave Friday for the East. B.

POSTAL CARD - ONE CENT.

United States of America.

THIS SIDE IS FOR THE ADDRESS ONLY.

ADISON, WI
AUG 22
M
95

Mr. Walter Deane
Jaffrey
N.H.

The Botanical Gazette A Monthly Journal of Botany: Edited and published by John Merle Coulter, Charles Reid Barnes, Joseph Charles Arthur. Established 1875. Subscription, $3.00 a year.

Madison, Wis. JUL 15 1895 189

DEAR SIR:

We beg to acknowledge with thanks the receipt of your late favor, ~~with enclosure of~~ and to say that the regular edition of the Gazette is 550. Order your extra plates from Meisel, as many as you want for yourself & Rose. We will insert the & text in cover. — We do not think the name absurd & are pleased to publish the n. gen. —

JUL 17

Yours truly,

THE BOTANICAL GAZETTE.

Per CRB

Rose has marked MS. "60 separates"!

POSTAL CARD - ONE CENT.

United States of America.

THIS SIDE IS FOR THE ADDRESS ONLY.

Mr. Walter Deane
Whitefield
New Hampshire

Mountain Cottage.

The Botanical Gazette: A Monthly Journal of Botany: Edited and published by John Merle Coulter, Lake Forest University, Lake Forest, Illinois; Charles Reid Barnes, University of Wisconsin, Madison, Wisconsin; and Joseph Charles Arthur, Purdue University, Lafayette, Indiana. + + Established 1875. + + Subscription $3.00 a year.

Office of Publication, 616 Lake St., MADISON, WIS.

OCT 31 1895

My dear Deane:-

I hope you do not feel, as you have a right to feel, that I was almost rude to you and Mrs. Deane at Springfield - While my actions might bear such an interpretation nothing could be farther from my desire and thought as you know, I feel sure. I thought every day that I would get around to Mrs. Owen's to see you socially and to make your host's acquaintance; but one thing and another put itself before me that "needs must" be done, and so the time for my departure came and I had not really had an even short visit with you. After the adjournment of the Botanical Section I remained in Springfield a whole day, but I sat down in the writing room immediately after the morning Council meeting and did not leave it except for meals until 6 o'clock. In the evening I did go to the VanBrunt lecture on Wild Flowers (which I hope you + Mrs. D. enjoyed) - Then, before that was out, I went to the Council meeting which adjourned at 1:30 a.m. As all the cars had stopped running at that unholy hour I had to foot it 1½ miles to my stopping place

The Botanical Gazette: A Monthly Journal of Botany: Edited and published by John Merle Coulter, Lake Forest University, Lake Forest, Illinois; Charles Reid Barnes, University of Wisconsin, Madison, Wisconsin; and Joseph Charles Arthur, Purdue University, Lafayette, Indiana. + + Established 1875. + + Subscription $3.00 a year.

Office of Publication, 516 Lake St., Madison, Wis.

I rose at 6 the next morning to take the early train to New York.

That day was a pretty fair sample of my week which was neither restful nor profitable except the ante-Sunday part of it. I am sorry that your first experience with the A.A.A.S. was so unfortunate. I never saw the botanists — and for that matter almost the whole association — go to pieces so badly. Part of this was due to the very scattered accommodations at Springfield and their over-zealous provision for excursions. But if you will plan to come to Buffalo I think I can assure you a much better meeting and a jollier time. We do things better in the West, you know! (Wednesday Am.)

After leaving the A³S. I went to N.Y. and had a day in the Columbia College Herb^m with Mrs. Britton. I also stopped over a night in Washington and then went on to West Va. where my wife was staying with our relatives. For two weeks I did absolutely nothing but eat and sleep, ride and read novels! Chickens and melons, apples and grapes, milk and cider, with intervals of hammocks and Hope, Stevenson, Maclaren and Dumas — I wish it might have been a month!

The Botanical Gazette: A Monthly Journal of Botany: Edited and published by John Merle Coulter, Lake Forest University, Lake Forest, Illinois; Charles Reid Barnes, University of Wisconsin, Madison, Wisconsin; and Joseph Charles Arthur, Purdue University, Lafayette, Indiana. + + Established 1875. + + Subscription $3.00 a year.

OFFICE OF PUBLICATION, 616 LAKE ST., MADISON, WIS.

Of course I had to pay the fiddler when I got home, for I found the Sept. Gazette stalled & a stack of mail which entirely covered my desk! I am just getting "caught up" now. —

So now at this, really my first, opportunity I want to apologize for my seeming neglect and tell you and Mrs. D. that I am as sorry as I can be that I did not get to see more of you. I am serving my sentence in the secretaryships of the A.A.A.S., It will expire next year: then I shall be free again I hope to mingle with my friends —

As to the separates, I am very sorry that they did not receive covers. We are charged for covers by printers and I will inquire into the matter and make them deduct. Of course you are to deduct $1.00 from bill. By the way how did you come out on the Deanea plates? We retained 550 copies but as some nos. had been sent out as samples, had 15 over, which we send you — Maybe you can use them —

With kindest regards to Mrs. Deane, in which my wife joins me, Cordially yours, C.R. Barnes

The Botanical Gazette: A Monthly Journal of Botany: Edited and published by John Merle Coulter, Lake Forest University, Lake Forest, Illinois; Charles Reid Barnes, University of Wisconsin, Madison, Wisconsin; and Joseph Charles Arthur, Purdue University, Lafayette, Indiana. + + Established 1875. + + Subscription $3.00 a year.

OFFICE OF PUBLICATION, 616 LAKE ST., MADISON, WIS.

NOV 5 1895

My dear Deane:—

In looking up the cover question I find that your Notes III, covered by our bill dated Oct. 12–, were covered ~~by~~ also by the printer with our usual stock. You probably thought the charge was for separates of Deanea which were not covered. Although by my carelessness, we were obliged to reset that article to furnish the separates ordered we shall ask you to accept the same with the compliments of the editors. This is a "reward of merit" you see, for furnishing plate.

But we shall have to let our charge of $1.50 for covers of Notes III stand.

Cordially yours,

C. R. Barnes

Let it go now until we send bill for Notes IV.

B

The Botanical Gazette: A Monthly Journal of Botany: Edited and published by John Merle Coulter, Lake Forest University, Lake Forest, Illinois; Charles Reid Barnes, University of Wisconsin, Madison, Wisconsin; and Joseph Charles Arthur, Purdue University, Lafayette, Indiana. + + Established 1875. + + Subscription $3.00 a year.

OFFICE OF PUBLICATION, 616 LAKE ST., MADISON, WIS.

JAN 3 1896

My dear Deane:--

Coulter has forwarded your letter for answer. As to length of paper, ten pages is all right, though rather more than we were allowing. The half-tone portrait will be ready, and we shall reserve 10 pages in the February number. I regret that we could not print it in the January number, which however is over full as it is.

As to separates I hardly know what to say. We should like to furnish not only Mrs. Bebb, but you, with all you want, free. But I do not see how we can afford it. The plate will cost us about $12 and 125 separates would cost us $8.75 more. If we were making money off the Gazette I should be entirely willing, but as it is a 'tight squeak' to make it pay for itself we are simply obliged to cut the corners as close as possible, and ask our friends to share the labors as well as the glory with us. I think we shall have to ask Mrs. Bebb to pay for the pleasure of sending copies of your notice to her friends. We can send her 25 separates with plate and cover for $1.75. One hundred (25 free) will cost you $5.25 (and us $1.75). That we think is as near as we can come to carrying out our generous feelings in dollars and cents; though we will add to that our grateful acknowledgements for the preparation of the biography.

Yours ever C. R. Barnes.

These figures are on the basis of between 8 + 12 pages

P.S. What are you driving at these days? I have been hoping you'd write me about your new work. B.

My dear Deane:- JAN 16 1896

The MS. has arrived safe. I expect it to make more than 12 pp.—probably 14—but have not counted it or estimated carefully. But we'll get it in. May I modify it in a few spots—editorially, you know?

Yours Ever C.R.B.

FROM
C. R. BARNES
MADISON, WIS.

POSTAL CARD - ONE CENT.

United States of America

THIS SIDE IS FOR THE ADDRESS ONLY.

JAN
12 M
96

1

Walter Deane
9 Brewster St.
Cambridge
Mass.

THE BOTANICAL GAZETTE: A monthly journal of botany, edited and published by John Merle Coulter, Charles Reid Barnes, and Joseph Charles Arthur. ⁂ ⁂ Established 1875. ⁂

Madison, Wis. JAN 25 1896

Dear Sir:

We beg to acknowledge with thanks the receipt of your late favor.

~~enclosing~~ Don't be alarmed about your MS. I'll not mutilate it! I hesitate to send copy back with proof, because I have been caught by loss in mail & by delay. But at your urgent request I will send it. You must take the risk.

Yours truly,

C. R. Barnes.

POSTAL CARD - ONE CENT.

United States of America.

THIS SIDE IS FOR THE ADDRESS ONLY.

JAN 25 5 PM 96

Walter Deane
9 Brewster st.,
Cambridge
Mass

THE BOTANICAL GAZETTE: A monthly journal of botany, edited and published by John Merle Coulter, Charles Reid Barnes, and Joseph Charles Arthur. Established 1875.

Madison, Wis. JAN [illegible]1 1896

Dear Sir:

We beg to acknowledge with thanks the receipt of your late favor ~~*enclosing*~~ & to say that MS. will be sent as soon as set, & will probably reach you by Feb. 5. But MS. from printer is usually cut up into "takes" & much smudged in addition & we doubt whether you can use it conveniently for reading. Will send 2 proofs one of which you can use for this purpose.

Yours truly,

Bot. Gaz. B.

POSTAL CARD - ONE CENT.

United States of America.

MADISON, C. FEB 1 12 96

THIS SIDE IS FOR THE ADDRESS ONLY.

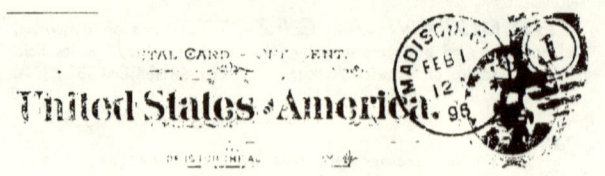

Mr. Walter Deane
Cambridge
9 Brewster st. Mass.

The Botanical Gazette: A Monthly Journal of Botany: Edited and published by John Merle Coulter, Lake Forest University, Lake Forest, Illinois; Charles Reid Barnes, University of Wisconsin, Madison, Wisconsin; and Joseph Charles Arthur, Purdue University, Lafayette, Indiana. + + Established 1875. + + Subscription $3.00 a year.

Office of Publication, 616 Lake St., Madison, Wis.

Feb. 18, 1896.

Mr. Walter Deane,

Cambridge, Mass.,

My dear Deane:-

The slip of name in announcing your memorial of Mr. Bebb was entirely my own. I was obliged to write the announcement when I could not get at your manuscript and I thought I remembered that Mr. Bebb's name was Moses. Greene of course is merely chaffing you. His letter does not indicate at all that Mr. Parish has mistaken the name. I return herewith Greene's letter. I shall be able to send you ~~reprints~~ separates very shortly now.

Mr. Bebb's family has ordered a hundred in addition to your own so that the paper will be pretty well distributed.

Yours as ever, Barnes

THE BOTANICAL GAZETTE: A monthly journal of botany, edited ~~and published~~ by John Merle Coulter, Charles Reid Barnes, and Joseph Charles Arthur. Established 1875.

Madison, Wis. July 6/96

Dear Sir:

We beg to acknowledge with thanks the receipt of your late favor enclosing MS. on Viburnum. Plate has also been received from Robinson. Probably can get into Aug. no.

Yours truly,

POSTAL CARD - ONE CENT.

ted States of America

THIS SIDE IS FOR THE ADDR... ONLY

Walter Deane, Esq.
Whitefield,
N. H.

THE BOTANICAL GAZETTE: A monthly journal of botany, edited ~~and published~~ by John Merle Coulter, Charles Reid Barnes, and Joseph Charles Arthur. ✠ ✠ Established 1875. ✠

Madison, Wis. MAY 23 1896

Dear Sir:

~~*We beg to acknowledge with thanks the receipt of your late favor enclosing*~~ If there are any typog. errors in your articles in Feb. & Apr. nos. please send corrections at once.

Yours truly,

C.R.B.

POSTAL CARD - ONE CENT.

United States of America

THIS SIDE FOR ADDRESS ONLY

MAY 23
8 PM
95

Walter Deane
9 Brewster st.,
Cambridge
Mass

UNIVERSITY OF WISCONSIN
MADISON, WIS., U. S. A.

BOTANICAL FACULTY
INSTRUCTION IN PURE AND APPLIED BOTANY IS GIVEN IN VARIOUS DEPARTMENTS OF THE UNIVERSITY BY THE FOLLOWING STAFF

CHARLES R. BARNES, PROFESSOR OF BOTANY.
EMMETT S. GOFF, PROFESSOR OF HORTICULTURE.
HARRY L. RUSSELL, PROFESSOR OF BACTERIOLOGY.
LELLEN S. CHENEY, ASST. PROF. OF PHARM. BOTANY.
RODNEY H. TRUE, ASST. PROF. OF PHARMACOGNOSY.
WILLIAM D. FROST, INSTRUCTOR IN BACTERIOLOGY.
GRANT SMITH, ASSISTANT IN BOTANY.

Dec. 30. 1897.

My dear Deane:-

I sent you this morning a booklet as a reminder of my good wishes for you and Mrs. Deane during the coming year. I fully expected such a reminder to reach you on Christmas and among my scanty Christmas shopping I included a little book for you. But I was obliged to be away at the time that it was to be sent, so I commissioned my wife to attend to it, telling her which volume, out of several I was sending, I designed for you. By a strange aberrancy of memory she inscribed two books to one of our friends and omitted to send yours; and when I got home I found that she herself had discovered the mistake. It was too late then to rectify it, so I thought best to wait until New Year's before writing my — pretty nearly annual now, is n't it? — letter, and sending the little token. Of course the omission is of little consequence when you are assured that it was not due to forgetfulness of you.

Things are going along in a very quiet fashion here. I am working hard this vacation to finish up the "tailings" of my little book for high schools, which is now in the press of Henry Holt & Co. I hope it will be published in the course of a month or two now. Then there will begin the revision of Plant Dissection, for which A.B.C. arranged just before Christmas. The thing keeps selling and is so sadly out of date that we are unwilling longer to have it bear our names without revision. That means practically rewriting. Of that I have the Bryophytes & Pteridophytes to do. We shall greatly increase the number of types, without ~~so~~ much enlarging of the book as a whole.

Some time between now & June I must do the Beauvois types of mosses (1805) which are now in my hands to the number of about 80. How I shall ever get through I do not see! —

Saturday (25th) was our 15th anniversary, which we celebrated by a reception to our friends, sending out about 275 invitations. I wish you and Mrs. D. could have been with us. Mary wore her wedding dress, of course, and a queer figure it made with the tight sleeves and panniers of 15 yrs.-old fashion. Her dressmaker was anxious to modernize it, but nothing of that kind is ever to happen! — Mary keeps well now, in spite of church work, clubs galore, and housekeeping duties. Lyle is such a big boy now you would not know him. 10 years old last Sept. and tall enough for 13. He's out ice-boating today. Skating & coasting both fine.

Mary joins me in warmest greetings to you both and heartiest goodwishes for 1898.

Ever sincerely yours, C.R.Barnes

September 6, 1898.

My dear Dean:-

You may be quite sure that it was only the old story of lack of time for all the things that pressed upon me, that prevented my writing to you in full in regard to me prospective, and now actual, move to Chicago. The matter has been hanging fire for a long time, simply awaiting the time when the University of Chicago was ready to develop its botanical department more fully. It seems possible to start that part this fall and so I find myself here trying to become oriented, and to get a new home settled. It was no small trial to us to give up our beautiful house and leave the delightful surroundings in Madison to take up our abode in a city which can lay few claims to beauty, except in its park system. We have taken a house only a few blocks from The University and, although it is large, compared with some others,

it seems almost impossible to get into it the numerous things that have accumulated in the course of our sojourn at Madison. We have been trying to cover floors intended for carpets with rugs that are too large for them and trying to stretch curtain poles that were too short to span the windows and door-ways. Then too we have accumulated so many books that it is quite impossible to find wall room for them in the new house. For the last week we have been sweltering in a daily temperature above 90 and have been able to do only a little work, just enough to enable us to eat and sleep in the house. It will be weeks before we are fully settled. I feel sure, however, that it will be more than that before you come west to visit your Chicago relatives and acquaintances, and I, therefore, do not hesitate to say that we shall be delighted to see you in our new house whenever you do come this way. It was a great disappointment to me not to be able to attend the Boston meetings last month. I had counted on renewing my delightful acquaintance with so many of the Cambridge people and not the least upon again seeing you and Mrs. Deane, but the meeting came just at a time that it was positively necessary for me to move, and I could spare neither the time nor the money for the eastern trip. I hope you enjoyed the meeting for you must have come in contact with many botanists whom you knew or had heard of. Mrs. Barnes keeps in reasonably good health and Lyle is doubtless grown beyond your recognition. Mrs. Barnes' sister, Mrs. Davidson, and her three children will make their home with us here. I hope Mrs. Deane is quite well and that her antipathy to long railroad journeys will not keep you from a western trip this winter. With warmest regards to you both, in which, I am sure, Mrs Barnes would join were she here, believe me,

Ever sincerely yours

C R Barnes

Mr. Walter Deane,

Jaffrey, N. H.

The University of Chicago

Department of Botany — The Botanical Gazette

December 31, 1898.

My dear Deane:-

I hoped that I would get time this vacation to write a letter in the way that you like to have them. But it is now the last day of the week and I shall have to put you off with a type written letter.

I received your package a day or two before Christmas and was delighted on opening it to find another volume of Burroughs's delightful books. All of them have been charming, and I am anticipating much pleasure from the perusal of "Pepacton."

We are beginning to feel as though we were not strangers in a strange land, and the new place is becoming a little more like home, as the memories of Madison begin to fade. Whenever we look back, however, we have much to regret in leaving that beautiful, and above all, clean town. Perhaps the hardest thing to get used to in the city is the inevitable dirt. I suppose after while we shall cease to try to keep clean, and accept the grime philisophically.

I am sorry to hear that Mrs. Deane is ill. There is a good deal of grip out this way, but so far, we have escaped it. Lyle is in bed with one of his bilious attacks, as the result of too much candy and nuts and general dissipation through the holiday week. Mrs. Barnes is quite well. Did I write you that her sister and three children are living with us now?

I shall be much interested in seeing a copy of the new journal, for which I think you have selected a beautiful name. I am very glad that you did not call it the "New England something," for lang names in references are a nuisance. "Rhodora" is appropriate, pleasing, and brief; three admirable qualities. I am sure Dr. Robinson will put a great deal of energy and skill into its editing, and I know that Rand will make the finanètal side go, if anybody can. However, it is likely to prove an expensive luxury for a few yeras unless there are enough of you to divide up the deficit.

Mrs. Barnes joins me in cordial greetings and best wishes for a Happy New Year, both to you and Mrs. Deane. Give my kindest greetings to Robinson, Rand, Churchill, and Kennedy when you see them.

Ever faithfully yours,

C R Barnes

Mr. Walter Deane,

Cambridge, Mass.

The University of Chicago

Department of Botany

The Botanical Gazette

December 29, 1899.

My dear Dean:— (I know you'll forgive the typewriting for the sake of the longer letter! Now that I have a stenographer I've forgotten how to do any thing but sign my name)

The charming little book which you sent came a few days before Christmas, and in accordance with your note on the corner was kept unopened until Christmas day. It is a delightful little story and

gifts. Although the fracture is a simple one, it necessitates a good deal of suffering for the first few days. She will have a plaster cast on it by Sunday and will then be able to hobble about.

Another distraction has been the meeting here of a group of naturalists who are about to form a western branch of the American Society of Naturalists. I have felt it necessary to be at the meetings and to do what I could to make the guests of the University at home. The absence of Dr. Coulter since July first has thrown all the administrative work of the Department upon me, as well as the giving of one of his courses, so that I have had much more to do than usual this year. That, together with the organization of the new laboratory, has kept me so busy that I have had no time for research work, and very little for play. Dr. Coulter will return April first, although he is entitled to three months further absence. He and Rose are working over the Umbelliferae again. He has also in hand a college book on the morphology of the seed plants and has published during 1899 his Plant Relations and Plant Structures, two texts in the Twentieth Century Series of the Appletons.

The photographs which I sent you were all taken at "Oakledge," our Summer cottage at Madison. It is about three miles and a half from the town on the south shore of the lake in a patch of oak woods. The shore of the lake there is a rocky bluff about twenty feet high. The picture marked "along the shore east," shows this bluff in front of our cottage. That picture is taken from the landing pier about a hundred yards from Oakledge. "The home I left behind me" is the house at Madison, 610 Lake Street. I sincerely wish it were 5733 Monroe Ave.! Some of the pictures were taken by Lyle, some by Mrs. Barnes, and most of them by me. All of them were taken last summer. The family left here

first six weeks of the Summer Quarter I lectured here on Mondays, Tuesdays Wednesdays, and Thursdays, went up to Madison Thursday evening and spent Fridays, Saturdays, and Sundays there. During the last six weeks, with the exception of two weeks in Ohio, partly at the meeting of the A.A.A.S., I spent at the cottage. It is a delightful place and we thoroughly enjoyed the change from the city.

Mrs. Barnes is very well these days and has been so for a considerable time. Her last illness of any account was a severe attack of the grip nearly a year ago. In one way and another, however, we have been running a hospital at our house most of the time. The middle of October I was attacked by diphtheria and Mrs. Davidson and her youngest boy, eight years old, were also down. Their cases were quite light and mine quite severe. We all had anti-toxin and the rest of the family were given an immunising dose. They escaped. The necessary isolation for three weeks and the fumigation of the house afterwards made it an experience not to be desired, although anti-toxin has robbed the disease of its terrors. Mrs. Barnes was chief nurse, although for a week we had a nurse from one of the hospitals. She stood the strain very well, although it made very hard work. This is the first time that I have been abed, except for an attack of the grip last spring, for about twenty years. My grip attack lasted only a few days, but this kept me in the bed for two weeks, and in the house for three.

I am much interested in what you tell me about Miss Horsford. I met both once when I was at Cambridge, but had not heard before which Miss Horsford it was. I knew of Farlow's engagement some weeks ago. I was of course as much surprised by it as any one well could be. In a recent letter I told him that he ought to have done this long ago! He's been there, and she's been there, lo! these many years!

you both again and enjoy one of the cozy chats in your library. Tell Mrs. Deane that Mrs. Barnes joins me in warmest regards and best wishes for A Happy New Year. In these sentiments you may be sure that you also share.

I quite agree with you that the twentieth century does not begin until another year, and refuse to be drawn into any controversy by that last remark of yours! — Do write me again and give me all the botanical news you can pick up at Cambridge. I find great difficulty in getting hold of the movements of botanists. Here I just learn that Piper has been for some months in Cambridge and Greenman is in Europe! But news ceases to be news after it is three or four months old. Wont you be my information bureau? You must pick up a lot of items at the New England Botanical Club. Let me have for the GAZETTE anything that is suitable to publish.

As ever yours,

C.R. Barnes

You've never told me what your "daily task" is now, nor anything about any "chest trouble". Do enlighten me—

Have recently written articles on Flower & Fertilization for Bailey's Encyclopaedia of Hort. Do you hear from him? I fear he's killing himself with work.

Give my best to all the botanical friends you meet— Robinson, Rand & Kennedy particularly! —— B ——

The University of Chicago

Department of Botany | The Botanical Gazette

December 31, 1900.

My dear Deane:-

I was hoping that during the Christmas week I should find time to write you a letter with my own hand, but have had to abandon that hope and resort now to a dictated letter, which I am sure you will forgive, since I can make it so much more satisfactory in content even than a written letter.

My little stamp box doubtless reached you somewhat behind time, as my Christmas presents usually do! It was impossible to me to get down town to get it until the day before Christmas. You know I invariably put off my shopping to the last minute; while, as your book evidenced, you had been forehanded as usual. Now that one has to stamp checks as well as letters, a pocket stamp box is not inconvenient.

I have not had opportunity yet to read the attractive book you sent, but I am sure from looking it over two or three times that it will prove as delightful as it is attractive.

The week has been a busy one here because we have had the second meeting of the Naturalists of the central states. About 70 or 75 people have been here, and in addition to the hours spent in the sessions we have been trying to entertain our friends by both social and university attentions. A considerable number of botanists were among the attendants. Ramaley from Colorado, and Jeffrey from Toronto represented the extremes, I believe. There were about twenty from abroad, and these with our own staff and advanced students made up a very respectable botanical section.

flower and fertilization. This autumn he has asked me to write the article on Teratology, and I am now getting ready for that. I am also interested in the revision of the International Cyclopedia and have been doing some preliminary work on that. The whole subject of botany is in charge of the department here and we are dividing it up among our men. Of course I shall have the physiological topics. Just as soon as possible I am going to get out a physiological text, something after the scope of J.R.Green's book, just issued. It will traverse rather different lines, however. This represents about the extent of outside work which I have been able to do this year.

On the first of July I was appointed one of the deans and have charge of the granting of advanced standing to students who come from other colleges, and the valuation of the work of graduate students who are candidates for a second degree. Being rather new to this administrative work, it has taken a good deal of time. It gives me, however, some additional compensation and, ex officio, more prominence in the various faculties.

We spent our summer at Madison as usual, that is to say the rest of the family did. Mrs. Barnes and her sister, with the children, were there from about the middle of June. Between the first of July and middle of August, I went up on Thursday nights and spent Friday, Saturday and Sunday with them. After the middle of August, I was there continuously until we returned late in September. We find our summer place as delightful as usual and it is always a pleasure to get back to Madison among old friends, of which we have many there.

Our recent Christmas gift from Mr. Rockefeller will redound decidedly to the advantage of the botanical department, as it provides for the erection of a press building, which will rid us of our tenants-at-will, the Press Division, who occupy one of our best laboratories and pretty much all of the basement for storage. As the new funds also provide for the improvement of the ground, it will enable us to finish our pond in the court and to plant it more extensively than we have yet done. Other buildings, ten in number, which are already provided for, and which are about to be begun, will remove from before out front door a low rough barrack like brick building which has been temporarily occupied by the gymnasium and library. The new students' club house will also relieve us of two temporary tenants, students' clubs, which occupy two of the good rooms on my fourth floor. So we grow gradually and I think as rapidly as sound development permits.

I was delighted to get your letter this morning and to hear how you are coming on. I only wish you had told me more about yourself and Mrs. Deane.

You have doubtless noticed that our changed address means new quarters. In April we moved from the three story house which we occupied on Monroe Avenue to the sixth floor of a apartment building where we have nine good rooms and two bath rooms. Mrs. Barnes's sister had been with us for the past two years, but when we returned to town in the autumn, she took apartments of her own a few blocks away, so that we are now alone. We like our new quarters very much and find the change a most agreeable one. The other quarters were a constant source of irritation; while the present ones are a constant source of satisfaction.

Are you not coming out to Chicago to see your brother some of these days? I wish you could. We should like to share in such a visit. Remember that you have a cordial welcome waiting you whenever you can come this way. Mrs. Barnes joins me in warmest regards both to Mrs. Deane and yourself. Both of the wives seem to have so much better health now that I think we may both congratulate ourselves. I hope we can increase this correspondence to a semi-annual one! Let us start out the new century aright.

As ever, Sincerely yours,

The University of Chicago

Department of Botany The Botanical Gazette

May 23, 1901.

My dear Deane:-

Your note of May 21 is at hand. So far as I am aware there is no possible way of predicting , except by a knowledge of its ancestors, what the color of any flower is likely to be. Certainly no one has discovered anything in seed or spore which enables this to be predicted. With a knowledge of the ancestors we know approximately what to expect, but in any given case there are variations which are entirely inexplicable. However, if Dr. Wesselhoeft proposes to base any inferences regarding animals upon the behavior of bulbs and seeds, you would better warn him that he is comparing structures which are not in the least comparable. Neither seed nor spore represent the sex cells and should he compare them to egg and sperm in animals he would simply be making a comparison which has often been made before, but which at the present day is utterly unjustifiable. I can't conceive how an allegation regarding the development of color in flowers could have much bearing upon the appearance of color in animals!

The color of a flower , by the way, is one of the last things to appear. It ordinarily does not develop until the flower is almost ready to expand from the bud. When we have discovered the physical basis of heredity for structure, we shall be nearer to a knowledge of why color patterns reappear in the progeny.

I am glad to hear from you and to know that you are well and busy. We have all been unusually well this winter and the visits of the doctor have practically ceased. He has hardly been in the house for any of us since the middle of last winter (1899-00). Mrs. Barnes had a little cold a week or so ago which shut her up for ten days, largely because she over-used her eyes and was compelled to protect them from the light and to avoid reading for some time.

At present we are in the throes of house cleaning and re-decorating. The house is torn up from end to end. (You observe that as we now live in a flat I do not say from top to bottom!) Mary would join me in kindest regards to Mrs. Deane and to you did she know I were writing.

Ever yours, C.R. Barnes

Mr. Walter Deane,

Cambridge, Mass.

The University of Chicago

Department of Botany

The Botanical Gazette

June 28, 1901.

My dear Deane:-

Your recent letter came to hand and I was much interested in your summer itinerary. My family have all gone to Madison for the summer and expect to be there continuously I shall be here until the last of August, except for occasional trips up. We have not quite so many places of sojourn as you and Mrs. Deane are to have , but the quiet retreat there seems to be just what Mrs. Barnes likes. She is impressed anew every time she goes back to Madison with the beauty of the surroundings and the kindness of the people.

I trust you will have a pleasant summer and return to work in the autumn with new enthusiasm and vigor.

What a splendid herbarium you have gotten together! I should think it would be almost a burden to house it now. I wish I could sit down with you and look over some of it once more. Perhaps I shall get east next winter. I am hoping to quit work and take a long vacation. I find that I am getting stale. Mrs. Barnes would join me in kindest regards to you both, were she here.

Cordially yours,

C R Barnes

Mr. Walter Deane,

Cambridge, Mass.

The University of Chicago

Department of Botany

The Botanical Gazette

January 8, 1902.

My dear Deane:-

I thought surely I should have time to write you during the Christmas recess, but it was completely absorbed by examination papers, reports, and a special job of writing whoch had to be completed by December 30. Then followed the meetings of the naturalists, at which we had over 300 , and these took all the days from December 30 to January 2 and a good share of the nights as well. We had a most successful botanical meeting , of which you will see a report in SCIENCE. Botanists were here from Minneapolis on the northwest, Denver and Dakota on the west and Columbus, Ohio to the east. At the other meetings , which the eastern societies had planned to hold at Chicago, of course there were many eastern men. Among them Minot, Mark, Sedgwick and others of that rank. I think they all had a good time, and certainly there was a surplus of papers.

The little book which you sent reached me the day before Christmas, and I have enjoyed its tales of animal life. Lyle is reading it also with interest. I think it in some respects superior to Seton's books. I gave Lyle "Lives of the hunted" and he has been devouring that nightly.

I carry the mate to the little calendar-diary that I sent you, and if your memory is as poor as mine, you will find it a useful affair. We should be twins that far at least!

Have I told you that we are going abroad for nine months at the end of this quarter? We plan to sail from New York on the 22d of March and I am almost counting the weeks until rest comes. I have been teaching almost continuous for three years and am getting decidedly stale.

I have nine months vacation accumulated and we shall not return until the last of December. I plan to be in Washington at the great meeting January first, 1903. Do make your arrangements to come down then. It is going to be the greatest gathering of scientific men of all kinds that the country has ever seen, for all societies both great and small are going to meet there.

We have all been thoroughly well during the past year, and Mrs. Barnes is actually getting fat. She weighs more now than she ever has and does a tremendous amount of going about. Sometimes she reaches her limit and has to slow up for a few days, but if she behaves herself reasonably she manages to do about as much as most people. She and Lyle and her sister and her family spent the summer at our Madison cottage and I ran up occasionally. I tried to spend September there, but about three days after I landed it began to rain and it rained continuously until the twentieth of September, except for one day, so that I had the pleasure of sitting in the cottage by a wood fire most of the time.

Except for these occasional breaks our life goes on in much the same round as usual. I wish I might see you before we go abroad. If you didnt "live so fur off" I might. Aren't you going to be in Chicago at all? I think you are very unbrotherly in never coming out to see Ruthven.

With warmest wishes for the new year, both to yourself and Mrs. Dean, in which Mrs. Barnes joins,

Believe me, ever yours,

C R Barnes

Mr. Walter Deane,

Cambridge, Mass.

The University of Chicago

Department of Botany

The Botanical Gazette

March 11, 1903.

My dear Deane:-

When I came home January 5 and found your note and photograph I laid the letter aside saying to myself that I would answer it at the very first opportunity. Unfortunately that opportunity seems to be further off now than it was then, for I am engaged in picking up the threads of dropped work and responsibility, and have hardly had time to sleep. When one is nearly a year behind the botanical literature he is in much the same fix as Barrie's man who was accustomed to read the _Times_ through every day and after an illness struggled manfully to catch up, but he never did! I fear I shall never catch up with botanical literature again. I have only time to say that we went through our nine months in Europe not only without serious illness, but with only that fatigue to Mrs. Barnes which occasionally compelled her to desist from attention to picture galleries and museums. She surprised herself and me by the amount of walking and sight-seeing which she did. We both enjoyed ourselves immensely and I came back thoroughly rested. Indeed according to my friends I am almost fat. At any rate, I feel thoroughly vigorous and ready for work. I was delighted to hear from you and to know something of your doings. Give our warmest regards to Mrs. Deane and say that we are not willing to surrender the hope that you and she will yet get as far west as Chicago to visit your brother and that we shall certainly expect a share of that visit.

Sincerely yours,

C. R. Barnes

Mr. Walter Deane,

Cambridge, Mass.

The University of Chicago

Department of Botany

The Botanical Gazette

DEC 23 1903

My dear Deane:- This is just a note to send you my Christmas greetings and to wish you a Happy New Year. You know you and Mrs. Deane are always in my thoughts, and especially at this season.

Unhappily the little token of remembrance (which I am making with my own hands!) is not going to be ready for Christmas, owing to a move & other time-consuming duties - But you will of course prize it the more the later it is! - Best wishes to you both -

Ever yours. C.R.Barnes

The University of Chicago

Department of Botany

The Botanical Gazette

December 26, 1903.

My dear Deane:- *Forgive this dictated letter! I am obliged to write it so or not at all, for ~~[illegible]~~ just getting off for St. L.*

The charming little book on Agassiz came to hand yesterday morning. I shall enjoy reading it hugely. I am going to take it with me to St. Louis tomorrow night, where I go to spend the week at the Science meetings. I have to preside this year at the B.S.A. Your Christmas remembrances are always so appropriate and so prompt that it quite shames your dilatory friend. I hope to be able to get off for you a package tomorrow night, but if I do not it will be delayed for a week or more by my absence.

We had a Christmas of the old fashioned sort yesterday, a heavy snow falling all day, and by evening a gale with a cold wave which sent the thermometer to minus ten this morning. My wife's sister, Mrs. Davidson, and her family dined with us and we spent a jolly day indoors. The children however, are getting so big now that one misses a great deal of the ecstatic joy of Christmas, but the quiet pleasures never pall.

I noticed that your package was addressed to my <u>earliest</u> Chicago residence! You people in Cambridge who "stay put" year after year do not realize what nomads Chicagoans are. In the five and a half years that we have been here we have lived in five places(!), which I admit is about as bad a record as even Chicagoans are apt to make. But the last three moves were due to our being away for nine months and then not being ready to settle down into a permanent place. We are getting ready to build a house, in fact I have the plans and specifications now on my table at home. We expect to break ground as early in the spring as the weather permits. A group of eight friends are going to build together. We purchased a large lot and have divided it up, planning to put six houses facing on one street and two on another, leaving the rear yards as a common garden, which we hope to make attractive. The group is one rather diversified in interest, which I think will make it all the pleasanter; one is a physician, one is a lawyer, one an astronomer, one a mathematician , one a philosopher, two philologists (French and Latin), and your humble servant a botanist. If you come out next October, therefore, you will find us, we hope, in our own house, and nothing would delight us so much as to see you and Mrs. Deane there. Apropos of all this, please correct your mailing list, and address me at the University of Chicago until that new house gives us a fixity that we have not had heretofore.

Just now we are occupying a furnished flat; some acquaintances wished to go to California for four months and as we were boarding we embraced the opportunity to have our own household once more.

Mrs. Barnes has been very well during the past year. Lyle, whom I think you never saw, is going away to school in January. He has done a little over a year's work here and so will enter the second year's work at Culver Military Academy. This is about 80 miles from Chicago and is said to be the best military school in the country. He is a particularly heedless and careless chap and I am looking to the military drill to straighten out that side of his training in a way that we have not been able to do. He is a little over 15, and is over 5feet 11 inches, in which you see he somewhat resembles his dad.

Botanical work goes along quietly. Coulter has been away for nine months and I have had a good deal of extra work on that account, but my chief burden nowadays is administrative duties in connection with a deanship in the colleges. I shall have to give it up I fear, as I see no prospect of reduction of work.

If we Chicagoans are nomands, you "Cantabs" are too much rooted to one spot. Will nothing induce you to come west? Is not your brother still in Chicago? Your botanical brother is, if your blood brother is not. I do wish we could see you and Mrs. Deane out here. I should delight to show you the University, for the "Grey city" is really well worth seeing.

Give my warmest regards to Mrs. Deane, in which Mrs. Barnes expressly wishes to join, and you will take your own share of course.

Cordially yours,

C.R.Barnes

306, 56th st.
Chicago, Dec. 25/0,

My dear Deane:–

As usual my Christmas remembrance to you is belated and has to be apologized for! But I've just been working my head off for the last two weeks getting ready my Philadelphia address as retiring President of the Botanical Society of Am., and really I could not give a thought to Christmas until yesterday. Then we searched the house for some photos I had taken some weeks ago. (You perhaps know that we've moved into a new house lately, which accounts for such mislaying). No pictures were to be found!

than it really has been, as we have had full possession for a month — so far as workmen were concerned. But the inefficiency of the furnace forbad the use of the lower floor until last week, when the entire heating apparatus was pulled out and another installed. Happily this one works perfectly and so we are now comfortable.

People who have lived in the same house for _n_ years (not to speak of people who keep the same cat for _n_ years) have no way of realizing the labor of settling in a new house when all one's household stuff has been in storage for 2 years

And they did not turn up until this afternoon! So I send it along, hoping that it will get to you by the time this letter does. Did I send you a copy before? I'm getting so addle-headed that I can't remember what I do and don't do—

I do wish I were going to see you at Philadelphia this week. Too bad of you not to come either to Chicago or even half-way!

We're quite ready now for that long-deferred visit of yours and Mrs. Dean's to Chicago. We have at last a house of our own of which I'm going to send you some views before long. I think I should have taken some long ago had my camera not been stolen. When Chamberlain (my colleague) went to Mexico after Dixon he borrowed my camera — a Hawkeye that I carried all over Europe — to take small pictures on his journey. While he sat down in the market place in a little town down there (near Jalapa) putting plants into his press, ~~some Greaser~~ he laid the camera alongside and some "Greaser" deftly abstracted it! He set the whole governmental machinery in motion to recover it (he had some special letters to high officials) but to no effect.

Well — the house. We occupied it in company with carpenters, painters, plumbers et al. — on Oct. 21. The last workman left yesterday! This sounds worse than

without attaining corpulency!)- She weighs more than she ever did, does a great deal of work daily & walks with a pace that a few years ago would have been impossible. Indeed since we returned from Europe she has hardly been even ill a day. So much, that is, to be thankful for.

I hope to hear as good news of Mrs. Deane, to whom especially Mrs. B. sends warmest greetings and best wishes for the New Year, though she does not forget yourself.

We have some hopes of going to Italy in April,

to Vienna in June for the International Botanical Congress, and the Tyrol for the summer. But that may not be possible. Will you join us if we go?

University matters go along smoothly. I hope you don't believe of the University what you hear in the papers. Most, if not all of the newspaper stories are absolute fabrications. We do try to be dignified, scholarly, and sensible, even if we do have some ideas that are not wholly conservative.

This is the twenty-second anniversary of our wedding as well as Christmas. Congratulate us on so long and happy a "dwelling together in unity".

As this pen is on the verge of giving out I'll stop. I'm looking for your Christmas letter tomorrow.

Ever yours most sincerely

C.R. Barnes

As I know you always read my letters to Mrs. Deane, as I do yours to Mrs. B., I have the one message and subscription for you both. May the New Year bring you all possible joys & satisfaction. B.

I got a glimpse of some chapters in the Ladies Home Journal & thought I should get the whole thing & read it. I'm taking it along tomorrow on my way to Phila to read on the train.

Thank you, ever so much, my dear fellow, for your unfailing thought for one who cherishes as one of his pleasantest memories the many hours of intercourse in the Brewster st. house.

Mrs. Barnes keeps wonderfully well and strong. Under all the care and work of settling the house she has actually laid on flesh (You will remember she can bear a good increase and over. To have such an accumulation of Chicago dirt cleaned off, of woodwork & coverings renewed is a work of time. And when your Penates are ready for installation the hangings & decorations of their temple requires much consultation, long planning & deep contriving — if your means are limited.

But at last most of the work is done, though there are some rugs to go down & some pictures to go up. Now comes the pleasure of having a house that you can stay in x years! (We're now looking for the cat.)

And to have a home-like place where your books are, and a dining room where you can gather your friends is truly a great comfort. –

My wife's sister & her two children are living with us this winter. Her eldest son who is at the Univ. of Wis. for his first year is home for the holidays & so is her boy who is at [illegible] Military Academy.

(That fountain pen is empty, so here is another!)

By the way, did you see that picture of Gibson's in Collier's Weekly for Dec. 10, having the title "Home for the holidays"? If not get a look at it – It's capital & of course we specially appreciate it. With our two boys we have seven in family. Last night we added five and had a little dinner of relatives. Our Christmas gifts were distributed this morning. A small tree on the breakfast table, a late breakfast, gifts from the family away & from one another in the household made a delightful Christmas for our first in the new home. Four young folks are enough to keep 3 older ones lively –

Not least by any means was the delightful book you sent as a Christmas reminder.

to the Bergens was a visit to Delpino, whom we found very feeble. We were shocked to hear of his death only a month later.

From Naples we went to Rome, stopping only a few days, as we had given some weeks to it on a previous visit and wanted the time for Florence. On the way thither we took side trips to Orvieto, Perugia, and Assisi to see the churches and early art.

At Florence we arranged to live with an Italian family, in the hope that I might get some practice in speaking Italian. But this "panned out" poorly, as the landlady seemed unable to speak "easy" — she always addressed me in a low rapid utterly idiomatic Italian which I could not understand at all. Her son, however, a young student in the R. Istituto Studii Superiori, and her brother, an employee in the cartographic

306 FIFTY-SIXTH STREET
CHICAGO

January 3. 1905.

My dear Deane:—

You may be very sure that my thoughts turn Cambridgeward much oftener than when I send you my annual remembrance and my annual letter. Whenever I see anybody from your region I inquire for Deane, Kennedy, et al., whom I remember with so much pleasure. Greenman is here now and still keeps up his interest in Cambridge affairs. And Robinson gave me a good account last summer of your doings — occasional at least — at the Herbarium and at the New England Botanical Club.

My doings for the year? — — It's a big contract, for I had

delightful summer abroad, filled with interest.

We sailed early in April by the Southern route landing for a few hours at Gibraltar, after a vision a day before of the beautiful Azores. We went all over the town and as far into the fortifications as the regulations permit. The harbor is magnificent and England's show of sea power and land is very impressive, though we could not resist the impression that there was more show than substance. The queer mingling of nationalities in the town — Spaniards, Moors, Tangerines, English, and Americans —, the odd costumes and customs, the delicious fruits — the sweetest oranges from Valencia and strawberries galore — made a lasting impression.

Landing at Naples, we came early into the famous bay, with so much mist and fog shrouding the shore that we were disappointed in the view. Landing was a slow ceremony, as it was done in small boats. The authorities allow this imposition on passengers to preserve to the boatmen their long cherished perquisites, though there is no reason why docks should not be built and used even by the largest ships.

We expected to find Naples so warm as to require summer clothing, but the weather was so cold that our winter flannels were none too warm. We stayed about Naples two weeks, including the usual excursions along the shore and islands. The Bergens were at Naples or rather Pozzuoli and did much to make our stay pleasant. We are so sorry to hear of Mrs. B.'s serious illness, which B. writes me, has so far prevented his visiting the west. We are hoping to see him next month.

Among our pleasures owed

at our ease to the evening band-concerts. But we had to leave to reach Vienna in time.

I won't describe the Congress to you. I exhausted myself on that topic in the July Gazette. We Americans had a good deal of fun over the "Dutch treat" style of the entertainments. Almost every night we were invited to some Café or Garden, where we paid for our beer and Wiener Schnitzel. As I wrote Coulter, if we had been entertained much longer I should have been bankrupt.

And we couldn't "get on" to the styles at all! Sunday evening a reception was announced as the informal opening at one of the City clubs. I refrained from going because I had no "claws". (Our trunk had been sent by freight from Naples and as we arrived late Saturday night we had not been able to get it.) But Arthur went duly attired as were the other Americans. But they found everybody in business dress. Next morning at 10 a.m. all we Americans appeared at the formal opening in the Fest-Saal of the Univ. in grays + browns. But our German + Austrian confrères were attired in claw-hammer coats, silk hats and a full expanse of shirt front + white tie! Finally we discovered that the hour was nothing: the formality of the occasion was the determinant.

We were left most woefully without directions. E.g. we were invited to a Friday evening entertainment—an Akademisches Gartenfest at Hittorf in Somebody's Brauhaus Garten. No map—no directions for reaching the place. Imagine yourself at the Faneuil Hall and expected to find a garden in Newton, four blocks from the ~~terminus~~ Ry station of the terminus of the electric street railway! You must find your suburban station or your carline + then hunt your garden!

The ladies were taken in hand by a committee of Viennese ladies who entertained them so continuously that by the end of the week they (+ their pockets) were total wrecks.

But the affair was most enjoyable, and I hope profitable. I hope nobody will kick over the traces now, but I fear it. The reports will be out this month or next at latest.

From Vienna we came to Dresden just for a few days — chiefly to see the Sistine Madonna once more, not to mention our dear old cross-grained kind-hearted Fraulein Bloch, who keeps a charming garden and an excellent pension and was most kind to Mrs. Barnes when she was ill there in 1902. Thence we to Berlin, where our son joined us, coming over by himself to Bremen after the close of his school work. Mrs. B. fell in love with Berlin and as Lyle liked it also (neither had been there before) we staid all of July. Charming weather — only 2 hot days — a jolly American picnic at Grunnau

bureau of the army, would speak clearly and slowly, so that I managed to make out their meaning pretty well. At any rate I got a good deal of knowledge of Italian, so that I can read it readily — but I never hope to acquire the real *finesse* of the language.

Of course we saw Florence pretty thoroughly this time — we had only given it two weeks before seeing over again the choicest things and taking in what we had missed before. Just before leaving F. we went over to Siena, where we spent several days most delightfully. Thence to Venice, for a hasty glance at some of the best things. Last time we staid on the Grand Canal; this time in a house on Piazza San Marco, a balcony from our room overlooking the Piazza, whence we could study the façade of St. Mark's and listen

Jordan's secy to say that... J's absence letter had just arrived from Coulter dated Milan, saying that he'd found books there & w'd send biography Ms. to Henry Holt & Co. by Jan. 1! Now, wouldn't that jar you! No letter from J. yet. Wonder what he'll say?

B.

on the 4th — fine music at the Gardens — beautiful parks — the cleanest, brightest, best managed capitals in Europe. Engler was most kind and Kny also. E. had us all out one Sunday afternoon to tea & showed us over the new garden himself. Robinson, Underwood, Lopriore & ——, ass't director Buitenzorg Gardens were in the party. Kny had us all to dinner in his charming villa in Wilmersdorf. (Wiesner also in Vienna.)

The first half of August we spent in Holland — Amsterdam (where I renewed acquaintance with DeVries) with runs out to Marken, Vollendam, Edam, Alkmaar (the cheese market of N. Holland) by tram and canal — thence to Haarlem, Hague, Scheveningen, Bruges, Ostend, Flushing, Middelburg, &c. — all quaint & interesting

Dutch towns, except the Cosmo-politan watering places, of which Ostend was the climax.

Then to Paris for a month & home.

Coulter & Cowles are both away & I've been over ears in work ~~that~~ quarter & have more in sight this quarter! The Gazette alone is a big job nowadays.

Mrs. Barnes is in fine health. She is so fat (!) that some of her acquaintances hardly know her! (As she only weighs 115 you will see that she is not too big!)

Glad to hear that Mrs D. too is well. We're still looking forward to that visit. Do plan it some time. I want you to see our house & the Univ. and above all I want to see *you* and *Mrs. D.*

Mrs. Barnes joins me in warmest regards to you both and best wishes for the New Year.

My special thanks for the "Old Fashioned Flowers." — "Delighted" — as T.R. says. Ever Your devoted Barnes

Ha! I thought I *had* to quit at the end of paper & lo! there is yet more.

But doubtless you've enough to last you a year!

By the way, when you get a bit of botanical news about anybody, of interest to the botanical public, drop me a note for the Bot. Gaz.

Must tell you that I've been working like a dog this vacation on a bit of biography of Gray which JMC once agreed to write & then abandoned when he went to Europe. Editor (Jordan) finally persuaded me to take it up! Just as I was ready to dictate the stuff comes a letter from

snow capped peak looks rather impressive and the shadow of the clouds on the lower range gives a good effect.

Orizaba is the highest peak on the N. A. continent (18,300 ft, except Mt. McKinley, and the in the tropics carries a snow cap of nearly 3000 ft.

I wish you could have been with us in September. You would have reveled in the semi-tropical vegetation that was so new to us. Us consisted of Drs. C. J. Chamberlain, W. J. G. Land, & Myself. We left Chicago on Aug. 30 and returned Sept. 28, going direct to Mexico city via Iron Mt. Route, Laredo, Monterey, San Luis Potosi. After a day in Mexico City we went to Xalapa, the capi-

305 FIFTY-SIXTH STREET
CHICAGO

Sunday, Dec. 23. 1906.

My dear Deane:—

I am sending you today some photographs of our Mexican trip, with which you may be willing to grace the doors of your herbarium cases.

The Alsophilas grow in abundance about Xalapa and gave a tropical air to the vegetation that of course impressed us northerners very much. These two fine specimens, one about 20 ft. and the other 35 ft. high, were photographed, only after clearing away the intervening brush — a half hour's job —, from the [illegible]

Interoceanic Railway. A third plant had been cut off about 8 feet from the ground (on which Dr. Land is standing) and as it still hung to the stump it gave me a chance to stand above Land's head and show the comparative height of the trunk & length of the fronds. The plant behind rose from much lower ground and towers above the smaller one.

We could not resist photographing Orizaba, which in the morning gleamed against a sapphire sky. The picture, framed in trees as one goes out the old Coatepec road, lava-paved, that issues from the southern plaza, greeted us every day as we went out to our collecting. We grew fond of it, and as our friends here seem to think it worth looking at I am sending you a print.

The third is sent as a curiosity tho it too is rather impressive." This was taken from the alameda of Xalapa, easily 35 miles from the peak. This plate is made by enlarging the part of an 8 x 10 plate on which the mountain shows of the size in the preceding. The detail of sculpturing is hardly visible on the plate, and the three craters are only specks, as you will see on the smaller print. The scale of enlargement would make the whole plate about 40 x 60 inches! Of course the mere specks become ugly blotches; but if you will set this across the room, the

that the origin, described for them by Leitgeb in 1880 and repeated by all textbooks of high and low degree for 25 years, is all wrong. One of the most instructive facts brought out in the investigation is the way in which Leitgeb twisted his observations to fit his desire to homologize the sex-organ pits & the air chambers— "We're all poor critters"!

Write me about yourself with your usual forehandedness. Your Christmas package came for me a day or so ago. I am hoping that this letter and my pkg will reach you Christmas morning— I was hoping too that I might see you in New York— That hope indeed included two mights: that I might go & that

tal of the state of Vera Cruz, via Puebla. The ride thru Texas was uninteresting and very hot. Nothing but chepparal from San Antonio to Laredo. Shortly after leaving Monterrey & Saltillo we entered the Chihuahua desert, which continued unbroken until we passed San Luis Potosi. Scattered plants, tree yuccas, cactus plains— gave a true desert aspect, so strange to unaccustomed eyes.

Xalapa is a town of about 20,000, where we had comfortable accommodations, lying about half-way down the mountainous edge of the central plateau where it falls off to the coastal plain. Thirty miles up or down the railway changed our level from 5000 ft to 8000 or 2000, so we had a great range of conditions within easy reach.

Our prime object was Dioon, which grown only in the neighborhood of Xalapa, and photographs of it <u>in situ</u>; secondarily we were to collect Bryophytes and Pteridophytes for morphological work; thirdly we were to lay in as many spermaphytes as we had driers for.

On all these counts our work was highly successful. Chamberlain got his Cycads — Dioon & Ceratozamia — pictures and materials for further research. Land took the pictures, by no means confined to Cycads, and good ones — 300 in number — they are. He & I laid in a lot of bryophyte stuff, particularly liverworts & Chamberlain got a quantity of the tropical ferns — Marattia, Aneimia, Gleichenia, et al — None of us ever saw liverworts grow before; the patches that we have thought luxuriant will seem mere starvelings hereafter.

I took in all the flowers that we could dry — all too few unfortunately — and they are now in Greenman's hands for identification. He tells me there are some interesting things.

But a truce to Mexico — I could write for days about it, for it was a new and most interesting experience to me — doubtless less so to my friends!

Nothing else has happened to me in the course of the year. Work has gone along slowly & surely. I have been working at odd times on the air chambers of Marchantiaceae, and have sent to the Bot. Soc. Am. this Christmas a paper showing

you might be moved to come down. But the first has failed and I shall be all the sorrier ~~if~~ what I lose in seeing others ~~of~~ is increased by your presence at N.Y.

I hear A.A.A.S. is to meet with us next year. I extend my invitation now for you and Mrs. Deane to make us a visit in the 1907 holidays - You owe it us, and doubtless you owe one also to your brother.

How is Mrs. D. these days? Mrs. Barnes is growing so fat that she can scarcely keep clothed. Not that she is huge yet, but 130 is an increase of about 25% which means a covering up of bones

that is more striking than it
would be in a plumper woman.
Withal she is very well and
also very busy keeping house.
We both join in the heartiest
Christmas greetings and good
wishes for the New Year.

As ever, sincerely yours,

C. R. Barnes

[Jan. 12, 1908] 306 - 57th st.
Chicago.

My dear Drane.

I am sure you have been wondering why you did not get your usual Christmas letter and some token of my continued affection. Perhaps you attributed it, charitably, to supposed absorption in the scientific meetings. At any rate I hope you have been trying to account for it on some other ground than forgetfulness. I have had, alas, only too good a reason for not sending you the annual letter at the right time and in

wanting. The case has at no time been dangerous, tho' annoying, serious, and as several "horrible examples" of acquaintances who did not take care of themselves properly have been here before my eyes, I have "been good". I have not even been propped up in bed, much less have I gotten up for a moment. Today ends the fourth week of my sentence, and at his visit today the M.D. was quite encouraging. He was even rash enough to say that he expected to be able to release me from the horizontal in two weeks more, if I conform as I have done the last week. [C. R. Barnes]

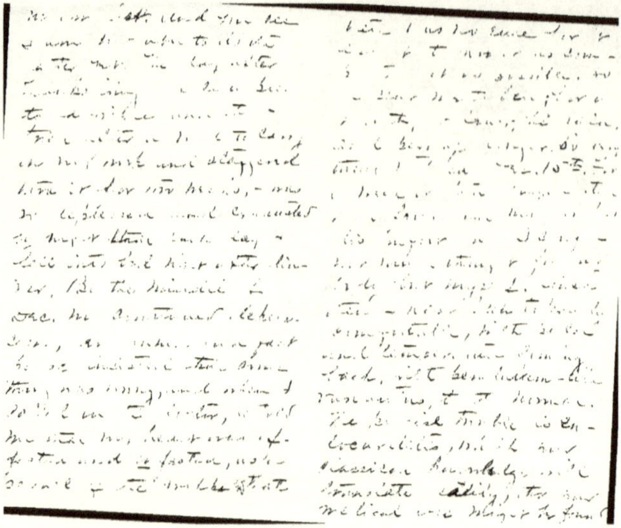

[illegible] weather, the summer and fall seeming [illegible] seasons. [illegible]!

[illegible] be mentioned because it carries a [illegible] of news. Dec. 25th was our Thirty-fifth anniversary and we [illegible] cards [illegible], but they [illegible] and the nursing [illegible] Mrs. Warner [illegible] time for [illegible] Xmas [illegible] [illegible] [illegible].

[illegible] wanted to see [illegible] away, and [illegible] [illegible] many [illegible]

Come, but it was not in [illegible]

[illegible]

[illegible] my time in writing & [illegible]

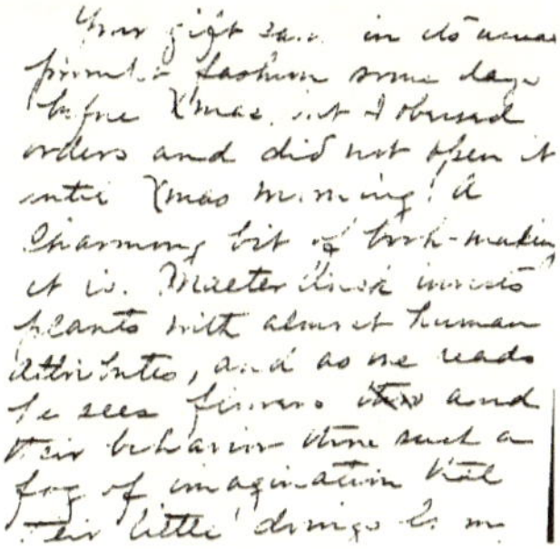
Your gift came in its usual
prompt fashion some days
before Xmas, but I obeyed
orders and did not open it
until Xmas morning! A
charming bit of book-making
it is. Maeterlinck invests
plants with almost human
attributes, and as one reads
he sees flowers and
their behavior through such a
fog of imagination that
their little doings to m

the year for she had a slight
attack of the grippe before I
got off! Fortunately there were
all [illegible] in [illegible] [illegible]
and she seemed to be quite
well. [illegible] [illegible] [illegible] and
Mrs Drum have [illegible] [illegible]
[illegible], [illegible] you [illegible] [illegible]
[illegible] wishes for the New Year.
[illegible] Mrs Barnes, who, as
you see, is [illegible] my
amanuensis, [illegible] cordially
joins. Write and let us
hear how you are and
what you have been doing.
[illegible] by your [illegible] [illegible] [illegible]
that you [illegible] in the [illegible] [illegible]
[illegible] report of you at
Xmas time

Yours most sincerely yours

E. R. Barnes
own his mark!

The University of Chicago

Department of Botany

The Botanical Gazette

February 12. 1908.

My doar friend Deane:--

Tho arrival of your kind note of acknowledgement and inquiry this morning reminds me of a duty that should have been attended to some days ago, when I first emerged from the helplessness of my 7 weeks in bed. Your letter and Mrs. Deane's, so full of sympathy and real affection reached me while I was still in durance and cheered me mightily. Will you think this "mechanical" letter a poor recompense for your concern ? Now that I am up again, it seems that there are more things to do than there are hours to do them in, and I can make a little time by using both hands instead of one to write to you.

I had my clothes on for the first time on February 2, and was allowed to walk around the second floor for a week before the doctor would let me go down stairs. Last Sunday he allowed me to go to church, which is just across the street, and Monday I had my advanced class (10 graduate students) come to the house for their first lecture. Yesterday I walked about six blocks and I think that by the end of the week I shall get over to the University, which is five blocks away. So you see that I am improving steadily and rapidly. The fact that it seems so to me is perhaps the strongest evidence of it. You've no idea how weak I was when I first put foot to the floor. There had been absolutely nothing, as I thought, and as the doctor assured me, in the illness itself to sap my strength, yet I could not stand up! Even when I was first raised to a sitting posture, my head swam. I would not have believed that simply the disuse of musclos for six weeks would have made them so useloss, at loast for a few days. Now, however, they are recoverimg tone so that I shall soon be as active as ever. I am warned, though, that I must be cautious about sudden strains on the heart for a year, by which time, the

Dear Doctor Robinson

This 1st page of Barnes' letter shows his condition now. The last sentence ends with "Doctor thinks the machine will be in thoroughly good running order again". He then goes on to other matters.

I have enjoyed much Rhodora for Jan— I rather expected a longer sketch of Mr. Davenport.

Sincerely

W. Deane

The University of Chicago

Department of Botany The Botanical Gazette

doctor thinks, the machine will be in thoroughly good running order again. I hope his prognosis is correct. I should hate to think of giving up tennis and hand-ball for good. I suppose I shall have to be content with golf this summer. I've always had it in mind when I was no longer really vigorous. I suppose, purely from the diagram you make of yourself, that you must use it as your form of outdoor recreation! Or are you too feeble for that ?

Sixty doesn't seem so old to me as it did once, and I don't believe you are sixty in anything but years, and they don't count at all except in statistics. I know I am only 30 in feeling, even if your record does say 50. I wish you would celebrate your birthday by making a visit to this western metropolis. You have no excuse now of being tied down by unescapable duties, and I surely think Mrs. Deane would find the journey as easy a the trip tp New Hampshire. Just think: you could get into a sleeper at 2 o'clock or thereabouts and be here the next evening, all the time with not enough swing or jolt to shake the water out of a full glass. And I'm not the railroad agent either! What a welcome the Barnes' family would give you! It would be the best in their locker, sure! COME!

Mary asks me to give you her love and say how much she appreciated your kind letters. She is a Martha--cumbered with much serving--or she would write herself. But she joins most cordially in that invitation, and as we have an excellent maid, the aforesaid serving is mainly outside--settlement, missionary, church, etc., that <u>can</u> be arranged.

My Salutations with my own hand, at least! You will hardly find in it any evidence of weakness or even nervousness, I flatter myself. I am writing daily now for a couple of hours on ~~the~~ book that must be done by Mch. 31, and must turn to <u>it</u>.

With much love to you both, Ever yours C. R. Barnes.

My dear Deane:--

I've just opened this letter again to say that since writing it I have found that I can't get off to New York as soon as I thought. I shall be delayed until Thursday, and possibly until Sunday, May 31. If you could spend Sunday with me there I would make it Thursday. We could run around, to the Garden and possibly to Cold Spring Harbor. You will get this in time to wire me if you can meet me in N.Y. Sunday. Do it, do it! It would be a lark (I hope) for you, and I assure you a great pleasure to me. You could run down on the night boat and come to the Saint Denis in the morning, where I would have arrived Friday night.

In the hope of seeing you face to face, and that soon, I subscribe myself again,

Ever yours,

Barnes

MAY 23 1908

if you could come down -
Maybe I could then carry
you off to Chicago!
Come if you can -
Ever yours
Barnes

Mrs. B. is O.K. Luncheon
yesterday: guests coming
tomorrow for over Sunday:
Church, Charities Board &
Settlement between times -
Occasionally works her-
self down, but we are
enjoying life hugely most
of the time - My love to
Mrs. Deane - Tell her
to send you to N.Y. -

[Recd May 25 /08]

THE QUADRANGLE CLUB

My dear Deane:-

Your note is just at
hand - I'm a beast for
not writing you earlier. But
shortly after the middle of
February I got into the
harness again, and when
I'm at work I do only the
things that have to be done
day by day, postponing
to a more convenient sea-
son (which never comes) many
things I'd like to do -

Oh, yes; I'm well & strong
again - I'm doing full work

but unfortunately I'm not doing full play! I'm debarred by the M.D. from tennis for this season. I'm thinking of taking to <u>roque</u> — do you know it? A sort of sublimated croquet! I had an examination a week or so ago — the first since I got out — & the Dr. found my heart in surprisingly good trim. In fact he thought at first that the murmurs had <u>entirely</u> disappeared, but finally was able to <u>catch</u> traces of the main one. He says I shall probably recover completely within 3 months, and gives his consent to our going to Mexico for the autumn quarter. Mrs. B. & I plan to go with Dr. & Mrs. Laud late in August and stay until Christmas.

I'm coming to New York Sunday night arriving at the St. Denis about 10 Monday night where I shall stay until Saturday night. Can't you run down for a night? I shall be free evenings and we could have a good talk. If I could possibly spare the time I would come on, but I must work (Gen. Edn Board, 2 Rector st.) during the days. I'd be delighted to see you.

new students and a new number of the Gazette — neither of which could wait — I had to postpone your letter. I might have dictated one — a note of acknowledgement, at least — but having "spoiled" a child, you must keep on. Besides I wanted to send you a picture or two as a souvenir of the old man — and so I kept on postponing the letter until I could send the picture. Then your letter caught me red handed in postponement — just as the transparency was done. I'm sending it tomorrow and hope you will be interested in my *pedestal* (which is *Echinocactus grandis* — or grande — which?) as it grows on the hills north and northeast of Tehuacan. I'm on it chiefly [illegible] show size, but incidentally

306 56th st.
Chicago, 7 F 09.

My dear Deane:—

You certainly have been treated shamefully this Christmas and I am indeed remorseful. But it has been thru no forgetfulness, I assure you. You know that Mary and I spent four months in Mexico, leaving Chicago September 1 and returning January 4. We came home by sea to New York, in order that I might attend the A3S meetings at Baltimore. We expected to arrive in New York Christmas day, but head winds delayed us so that we did not land until Saturday. We spoke of the letter due you on Christmas, and Mary urged me to write on the boat. But there was no stationery supplied us on the Atlantic liners, and it was such a bother to get in to the trunk

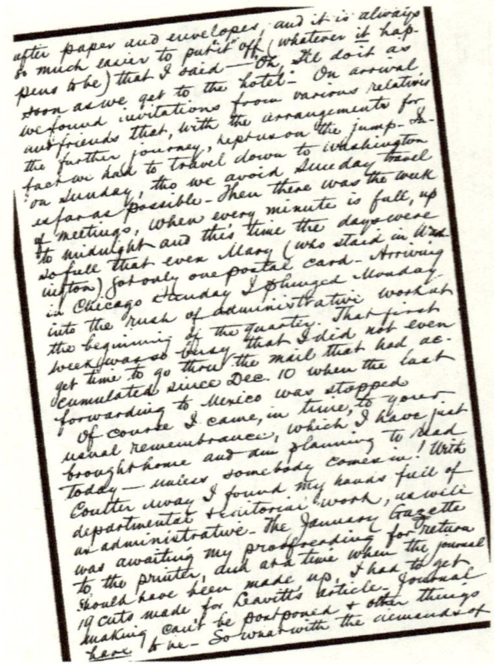

after paper and envelopes, and it is always
so much easier to put "it" off (whatever it happens to be) that I said — "Oh, I'll do it as
soon as we get to the hotel." On arrival
we found invitations from various relatives
and friends that, with the arrangements for
the further journey, kept us on the jump. In
fact we had to travel down to Washington
on Sunday, tho we avoid Sunday travel
as far as possible. Then there was the week
of meetings, when every minute is full, up
to midnight and this time the days were
so full that even Mary (who staid in Washington) got only one postal card. Arriving
in Chicago Sunday I plunged Monday
into the rush of administrative work at
the beginning of the quarter. That first
week was so busy that I did not even
get time to go thru the mail that had accumulated since Dec. 10 when the last
forwarding to Mexico was stopped.
Of course I came, in time, to your
usual remembrance, which I have just
brought home and am planning to read
today — unless somebody comes in! With
Coulter away I found my hands full of
departmental + editorial work, as well
as administrative. The January Gazette
was awaiting my proofreading for return
to the printer, due at a time when the journal
should have been made up. I had to get
19 cuts made for Leavitt's article. Journal
making can't be postponed + other things
have to be. So what with the demands of

I'm going to dictate a short story of the Mex. months and you can pretend it's printed & you're reading it out of a book. I could write as good a one as Hans Gadow's *Through Southern Mexico*, I'm sure. MacDougal is asking me to write something on the vegetation for Plant World, but I can't get time.

I'm sending you in the pkg. a paper on Marchantia that ought to have been written last May, and wasn't until Sept. in San Luis Potosi, where we had to wait 2 wks for our baggage & for Mrs. B. to get well of a dysentery. Thereafter she was O.K. & the paper was written, together with a dozen or so reviews (for which I had to carry with me the papers, having been unable to clear off my desk before leaving). Another case of an ill wind that blew some good.

You may like the portrait. If you take the trouble to look at this plant as pictured by MacDougal in his recent "Desert Vegetation" (Carnegie Publications) you'll see who can take the best photographs. I wish you could see our 400 lantern slides made from negatives taken on this trip. They're fine & I'm busy now talking about them — having nothing else to do.

Here by the way was last week's program:

Monday a.m., letters, proof, dep't business. 3 p.m. lecture, 6:00 Bios. club dinner to Conklin, ^ & his evening address.
Tuesday a.m. as Monday. 2 pm lecture; 3-4 office hours, 5 lecture. Evening at home reading proof.

Wednesday: am letters &c 11 a.m.–12:30 Bose (of Calcutta) to be shown around.
3 lecture – 4 Mendelssohn Centenary Concert (Thomas Orchestra) in Mandel Hall – 6:30 Dinner & Lincoln Celebration at Church

Thursday: am. proof & drawings for Gazette 2 pm lecture; 3–4 office hour; 4 lecture 6:30 Bose dinner at Quad. Club, 8 Bose address to biol. club in bot. bldg –

Friday: a.m. letters & business; closing Feb no. Gazette; 2 pm quiz, 3 quiz 4–5 office hour; 6:30 private dinner at Quad club (Greenmans), 8:30 at Club ladies night & lecture by Bryan on Kilauea –

Saturday: 8 am at office 8:30 – 11:30 fac'y & board meetings; 2:30–5 dictating letters (got thru half that had accumulated in Dean's office since Feb. 1) 6:30 dinner (our house) to Bryan of Honolulu:

Thank heaven, they aren't all like that! But they can be much less strenuous without leaving any real leisure. Last Sunday afternoon I planned to write you, but company all afternoon prevented –

Dear old man I wish you were near enough to talk to! We'd have a crack oftener than once a year I assure you. I want to tell you all about our Mexican trip, but I can't do it by pen. Stenographers have so spoiled me that I can't even write decently because I'm hurrying to catch up with what I want to say –

Land & I have another on the stock, the bulk of which was done and was presented at the 1907 meeting of the Bot. Soc. Am. We need to do a little more on it and heaven knows when I'll get time to write it up—

If you are around at the Garden tell Robinson that I got his letter about the 7th Ed. of Gray & haven't had a minute since getting where I could see the book to write & congratulate him on the job. But I <u>will</u>! He deserves the heartiest praise. The book is simply fine—quite out of sight of the rival one. Greenman, I fear, has been too modest to praise it enough in his forthcoming review (Feb. Gazette)– He even asked me

to tone it down if it seemed too fulsome
(because he had a hand in the work.)

When we went to Mexico, we rented
our house furnished to the Dean of our
Law school, who was building, had
to give up his rented house Sept. 1 &
expected to get into his new one Dec. 15. (Just a
lit, wasn't it?) But the new house, like all
others, did not progress as fast as its
owner expected, and it was Jan. 16 before
they were ready to let us have ours again.
For two weeks we had just a room with
one of our neighbors of the group, so that
we seemed to be still traveling. Wonder
if one could get the sensation by packing
his traps in a trunk and living in one
room at home? It would be cheaper.
Mr. Dooley, you know, proposed to get
upon the upper shelf of the closet &
put a cinder in his eye when he wanted
to enjoy again the delights of a Pullman!

Did you write me a Christmas letter?
What have you been doing the year?
Tell me.

Mary joins me in love to you both.
Remember your standing invitation. The
latch string is always out.

Ever yours C.R. Barnes

The University of Chicago
FOUNDED BY JOHN D. ROCKEFELLER
Department of Botany

THE BOTANICAL GAZETTE

May 27, 1909.

Mr. Walter Deane,

29 Brewster Street,

Cambridge, Mass.

My dear Deane:

Two weeks ago I sent you a box containing another transparency of the new species of Echinocactus, which Rose described, with very poor illustrations, in Contrib. U. S. Nat. Museum. I hope this will get to you sound. If not, it is hopeless to try to send such stuff, for this was thoroughly well protected.

I have been so occupied that I did not find the time to send you a letter announcing the shipment. I am doing my own work,, trying to revise the manuscript of a book, and getting ready over 1200 illustrations for it, besides carrying almost the whole burden of the Botanical Gazette. I should not have time to breathe if it were not automatic. If I had a chance, I should write you a newsy letter, but you will have to take the will for the deed, and remember that I think of you often even if I don't write . I envy you your relative leisure. If you would <u>only</u> use some of it in traveling out this way!

Peirce, of Leland Stanford, passed through Monday. He gave us a talk at the Botanical Club, and I gave him a dinner at our home, with a round table of ten botanists. We had a good evening.

Mary would join in sending love to yourself and Mrs. Deane if she knew I were writing.

www.ingramcontent.com/pod-product-compliance
Lightning Source LLC
Chambersburg PA
CBHW030001240426
43672CB00007B/778
9783337393953